ANDY GOLDSWORTHY

AT YORKSHIRE SCULPTURE PARK
31 MARCH 2007 – 6 JANUARY 2008

Exhibition generously sponsored by Roger Evans
with support from the Henry Moore Foundation

CONTENTS

INTRODUCTION
PETER MURRAY, EXECUTIVE DIRECTOR
YORKSHIRE SCULPTURE PARK

At the base of a sycamore tree there was a small, dark hollow where nothing stirred. A sudden flurry of movement and two eyes appeared, giving form to a face. A few grunts and a couple of agile twists resulted in a human form springing from this impossibly small space into an upright standing position on the muddy ground. It was September 1983 and Andy Goldsworthy was just about to complete his first work at Yorkshire Sculpture Park. The photograph resulting from this experience is titled Climbed into a rotten hollow. At base of a sycamore tree. Just enough room in which to turn and crawl back out. After which I worked the edge with mud. To make a black hole. The work emphasised the importance of the physical to Andy Goldsworthy and his long-standing preoccupation with the making of black holes. For him, the unfathomable depth of the hole is a window into the 'fragile, unpredictable and violent energy'[1] which he senses in nature.

In 1987 Andy Goldsworthy returned to YSP to undertake a three month residency spread over twelve months, enabling him to create a series of ephemeral works which responded to the changing seasons. In spring he made exquisite sculptures using dandelions, grasses, sticks and willowherb stalks. In summer he joined sweet chestnut leaves with thorns in a continuous spiral to make a green horn, and a memorable floating sculpture of iris leaves and rowan berries, which was attacked by fish from below and nibbled from above by ducks. Autumn brought a curtain of rusting sycamore leaves stitched together with stalks suspended from a still green oak, and his triumphant Trench, which took over two days to dig and build. It had the appearance of a jagged, dark, velvety line with the same unfathomable denseness as his black holes. In winter he wanted to make a Bretton snowball as well as constructions from ice. We waited and waited, but the snow didn't come, so Goldsworthy climbed into his battered Landrover and made the long meandering drive home to Dumfriesshire, only to be called back in the dead of night to work with a sudden flurry of snow. He often worked outdoors through the cold, dark winter nights, battling against the elements to create freestanding ice sculptures. On 20 February 1987 he constructed a mound of ice with a hole in the top which lasted several days, 'freezing at night, thawing during the day / growing smaller'.[2] This beautiful translucent sculpture may have signalled the later stone domes, which now occupy a space in the Underground Gallery. Few people saw these works, often hidden in undiscovered corners of YSP, but the results were recorded through the artist's compelling photographs in the publication Parkland, which has been reprinted to coincide with this exhibition.

These were exciting times for us all. We were learning about space, Goldsworthy was developing, refining and expanding his vocabulary, and together we discovered more about the riches of the layered landscape. Andy Goldsworthy's presence on site taught us much about the social aspects of the historic estate and the nature and experiences of the varied spaces. We benefited enormously from the innovative and perceptive qualities of this impressive artist and sensed the greatness which was to follow.

Since 1987 Andy Goldsworthy has travelled the world creating major works in Japan, Australia, New Zealand and many parts of North America. At Storm King in New York State, he made the Storm King Wall. Almost seven hundred metres long, like an undulating line it draws the shape of the land, dividing fields from wooded areas. At the National Gallery in Washington DC he made Roof – nine slate domes, each more than eight metres in diameter. These and numerous other private and public commissions reflect the international status that Goldsworthy has so rightly achieved. Often, however, the most exciting part of travelling, for him, is returning to smell and breathe the landscape of Dumfriesshire, where he has lived and worked for over twenty years. Moving to this part of Britain has had a profound impact on his work and his understanding of landscape. At home he has the right to roam. Here, he makes marks on rocks and challenges the forces of nature through projects such as the Burn Dam series, photographs of which are seen for the first time in this exhibition. Three decades earlier, working on Morecambe beach, Goldsworthy learned about the power of water and how the tide imposes severe deadlines. In the hills of Dumfriesshire the continued existence of his dams, constructed from the stones and timber of the burns, also relies on the mood of water.

As a student, Andy Goldsworthy was touched by performance art and North American land art. Studying at Lancaster provided immediate access to powerful countryside and views of the sea at Morecambe Bay. In his anthropometries, begun in 1960, Yves Klein dragged naked bodies, doused in paint, across canvases, and in 1971 Joseph Beuys immersed himself in a bog up to his neck to create Bog Action. In 1976 the young Goldsworthy dragged his own body across the sand and cold waters of Morecambe Bay in the performance work Black sand. Morecambe Bay, Lancashire. October 1976. He constructed temporary works on the beach and made marks in the sand to observe their gradual disappearance by the tidal movements of the Irish Sea. He experienced the exhalation of human air by spitting in the wind, and created momentary rainbows by thrashing river water in sunlight.

Performance laid foundations for future developments: stick throws are a good example. Carefully orchestrated performances resulted in throwing sticks into the air to form delicate patterns against the sky, before falling to the ground. In searching for more permanence for that fleeting moment, he experimented with leaf stalk screens, constructing the first at YSP in 1987. 'I tried to span what at that time seemed an impossible distance of at most 18 inches between two tree trunks and to my surprise succeeded.'[3] In the Underground Gallery he has made a screen spanning a twelve-metre space, comprising 10,500 horse chestnut leaf stalks collected from the Bretton Estate, held together with blackthorns.

Goldsworthy started working on farms when he was thirteen and identifies strongly with the problems and economics of rural life and the role of the farmer in the 21st century. His view of the landscape is tempered by his understanding of the underlying brutality of nature, its rawness and harshness, and by the intense and unforgiving labour of farming. He knows about ploughing and digging fields, lifting heavy bales, tending to animals, and mucking out barns 'several feet deep with shit'.[4] Cow dung on glass on the windows of Longside Gallery is a reminder of the relationship between green fields and the centuries-old tradition of agriculture and livestock farming in this part of Yorkshire.

For many years Goldsworthy has been fascinated by sheepfolds – used by farmers to manage flocks – and since 1996 has been engaged in making (and remaking) over fifty folds across Cumbria. He refers to folds as 'identifiable agricultural spaces – rooms in which farmers work'.[5] In collaboration with YSP's tenant farmer, Philip Platts, Goldsworthy has replaced an old wooden fold with a permanent stone sheepfold. This functional work of art also contains a large stone on which visitors are invited to lie down to view the sky or make a rain or snow shadow. On 8 February Andy Goldsworthy christened the YSP stone with his own shadow during the first significant snowfall of 2007.

His abiding interest in sheep, and particularly their often frenzied feeding habits, has also led to works such as his Sheep Paintings. Since 1998 he has pegged out large canvases in the fields near to his home. In the centre of the canvas he places a salt lick, observing the mark-making of the hungry sheep on the raw surface of the canvas. In 2006 he repeated this process with Yorkshire sheep in the Bretton landscape. A number of these large canvases are displayed for the first time in the Longside Gallery.

Planning this exhibition has taken several years and is the result of much research and discussion. We talked and walked the landscape many times; we looked at familiar and new sites, inspected old stone boundary walls and the 2.5 kilometres of often dilapidated historic ha-ha. We considered ways of bringing elements of the outdoors indoors and of rooting the exhibition firmly within the YSP landscape. We discussed our respective journeys; the growth of Yorkshire Sculpture Park and the development of Goldsworthy since his 1987 residency. Finally we agreed that the exhibition should reflect the artist's journey and achievements over thirty years and that it should also map a journey for visitors through YSP's 500 acre site.

Work started in February 2006 at Oxley Bank on the southeast boundary of the estate with the construction of Hanging Trees, which had its roots in a sculpture Goldsworthy made in California. In the grounds of the home of collector, Roger Evans, he built a house for a fallen tree which appeared to be suspended in mid-air. In Yorkshire, Goldsworthy chose to work with the ha-ha, which he described as an interface between the designed and the agricultural landscape. He selected three derelict sections of the ha-ha, excavated deep into the ground, and constructed three large, open, stone chambers with a suspended tree in each. The works reflect Goldsworthy's concern with the tension between stone and wood, 'a flashpoint of friction between two elements'.[6] Hanging Trees not only opened up a new perspective on the landscape, it set the tone for the gargantuan efforts required to realise YSP's most ambitious project to date.

Indoors, Goldsworthy has transformed the Underground Gallery, creating a series of breathtaking site-specific works, including the extraordinary Wood Room, a self-supporting structure made from coppiced sweet chestnut. The mesmerising Clay Room is a work of deafening silence which masks the huge industry of creating such a profound installation. It started in the ground; twenty tons of clay dug here at YSP, processed on site and then mixed with three hundred litres of cut human hair collected from local hairdressers. From excavation, through processing to completed installation, YSP staff, the artist, his assistants and over sixty volunteers, laboured for three months to create a perfectly plastered wall which has erupted into a naturally cracked, but stable surface. This compelling work blurs the distinction between the building and the earth: as if the ground has 'risen to the surface as a memory of its origin'.[7]

Since 1976 Andy Goldsworthy has produced a remarkable body of work, from the ephemeral to the monumental. He touches nature; he has made sad and poignantly moving images reflecting its raw brutality, and created huge, unbelievably complex structures from wood and stone, stalk and clay. For him, contact with the dynamics of the changing landscape is essential, rather than what he calls the 'dead space'[8] of the studio. The physical act of making is paramount, and this has been a vast project, both conceptually and physically. It has required huge commitment and dedication from stone wallers, numerous crafts people, skilled assistants and, critically, the artist, who was involved in every part of the process. The image section of this publication aims to capture the flavour of the making of the exhibition from February 2006 to March 2007.

In January 2007, art historian Tina Fiske interviewed Andy Goldsworthy: reproduced for the first time here, this wide-ranging dialogue provides a fascinating insight into the evolution and complex nature of his work through a perceptive analysis of recurring themes, ideas, philosophical rationale and the social context which fuels him. Goldsworthy's voice is clearly heard, articulating his ideas, as Fiske examines what drives and sustains him, his values and how he prepared for one of the biggest challenges of his career at Yorkshire Sculpture Park. Sensitively and skilfully judged, the dialogue directed by Fiske enables Goldsworthy to reveal much about his approach to making, in turn contributing greatly to our understanding of the significance and universal nature of his art.

Perversely, although Andy Goldsworthy is one of Britain's best loved contemporary artists, relatively little is known about his real achievements. As Tina Fiske points out, people don't have access to a large part of his work, except through books and photographs, which necessarily divorces it from its context. It was our aim to redress this issue by presenting a context for every aspect of Goldsworthy's practice. We would like to thank Andy Goldsworthy and Roger Evans for making this fascinating project possible.

In his Guardian review, Richard Mabey wrote, 'Simon Schama suggested in his TV series Power of Art that great art is the exploration of what it means to be human. Goldsworthy has a more inclusive take – he is exploring what it means to be alive.'[9] The Yorkshire Sculpture Park exhibition, and this publication, set out to convey the remarkable achievements of a truly extraordinary artist.

ENDNOTES (see Selected publications for full citations)
1: Stone, p64
2: Parkland, p14
3: Diary note from Goldsworthy's sketchbook
4: Andy Goldsworthy at Yorkshire Sculpture Park, p16
5: Ibid., p36
6: Ibid., p80
7: Time, p8
8: Andy Goldsworthy at Yorkshire Sculpture Park, p16
9: Richard Mabey, The Lie of the Land, pp12-13, Review, Saturday Guardian, 31 March 2007

ANDY GOLDSWORTHY
IN CONVERSATION WITH TINA FISKE

DUMFRIESSHIRE, JANUARY 2007

AG – Andy Goldsworthy
TF – Tina Fiske

TF: Can we talk about the influence that agriculture and farming have had on your practice? I'd like to consider it in terms of your ephemeral practice, and your permanent and commissioned works. It seems to me there are various layers to how you think about the land, and how you understand it. Those layers that you talk about most are the geological and the agricultural, the latter being as much about the human presence in the landscape. Your methodology as an artist, as well as your emotional and conceptual responses to the land, come out of a reading of the farmed landscape and you have often spoken about your sculptural appreciation of certain farming practices. Perhaps you could begin by talking about your experiences when working as a farm labourer?

AG: I began working on farms when I was thirteen. The farm was the place where I learned how to work with materials, equipment, how to work with the land and the fields. I worked on a dairy farm, and my first job was to wash milk bottles every evening. That had nothing to do with the fields of course, because I was inside. I still remember adding caustic powder to the water in one vat that washed the bottles, then lifting a lever to release the crate. It was a continuous, physical, repetitive process. As I speak to you, my body still remembers the motions, the process. At the end of the washing, each bottle had to be turned upright, so that the whole cycle could begin again the next day. There was a rhythm and skill to doing that. If you smashed a bottle, you had to start that crate again because there was glass everywhere. You learned how to pick up a crate, to lift two crates at once, to speed up the job. It took about an hour every night to do. I can still remember the large rubber gloves I had to wear, and the sensation of them leaking. The cleaning fluid would burn your hands.

TF: You did that every day?

AG: Every night, and then at the weekend. On Saturdays, my brother John and I would help on the farm, and that would be more in the fields – feeding the cows, mucking out. I did a lot of mucking out; I mean, cows shit a lot. You put them inside every day, and feed them when you're milking them, and they shit, and you have to scrape it all clean.

TF: At that time, you were living in suburban Leeds, on the edge between rural and urban. How did you view that then? Were you conscious of it?

AG: Grove House Farm, where I worked, didn't fit into the conventional idea of a farm. It was located at the interface between city and country. There is often something raw about interfaces, a tension. I lived to the west of Leeds, five miles from the centre. On one side there were fields, and the other, city. We moved when I was eight years old to a newly built house at Alwoodley. The suburb was expanding; ours was the latest house to be built. There were woods and bogs, which I played in with my friends. The woods were eventually cut down, and the boggy ground drained. I remember feeling angry as these places were cleared for development. But, as my friends reminded me, my house now sat on land that they once played on. I wanted to live there, so how could I deny someone else? When more houses were built you never quite forgot the woods or bogs that had been there before. So it had a profound effect on me, the relationship between the city and the countryside. Beneath that veneer of tarmac, I felt the swamp was still there. Farming itself is an interface, between people and the land. It's the front line. The experience of growing food, not in a kind of romantic, organic farm situation, but one that was at times brutal and industrial – planting and cropping with machines – that was a very powerful experience. Working in those early years on the farm I saw cruelty and brutality.

TF: Then you went to art school. Bradford first, and then Lancaster. How did the farm labouring sit alongside that? Did the labouring continue while you were at Bradford, or influence how you worked outside in those early student days?

AG: When I went to Bradford, for my Foundation year, I moved onto Grove House Farm. My parents left Leeds at that time, and the farmer [Christopher Carling] arranged for my brother John and me to live in a caravan on the farm. I lived there during the latter part of my Foundation, and during the holiday periods of my degree course at Lancaster. I loved having my own place and being able to earn my own money. The farm was a means to give me independence, but it changed from dairy to mainly grazing – sheep and cattle. That meant there was less work for me. So I started work on another farm near Bardsley, two or three miles away, and the farmer, George Cornforth, used to come and pick me up and take me to work on his place during the holidays and at weekends. That had arable farming as well as animals. So I did a little bit of everything there: bagging potatoes, picking stones, weeding, stacking bales, tending to sheep, mucking out sheds several feet deep with shit. It was like geology, you had to work it off layer by layer, sometimes finding dead birds and animals buried in there. I vividly remember the mad rush of hungry sheep – I once took a photograph of two dead sheep covered in mud, trampled in the frenzy of feeding. Farming provided very powerful images of animals, death, crops, as well as smells and textures. It was an incredibly sensory sort of experience. When I regularly began to make work outdoors during the first year of my degree course at Lancaster, I realised very quickly that the studio is such a dead space. There is death in the field, but that gives way to growth. I felt that the studio was suspended from that process of life and death. It was very difficult to get some motivation, to know why I was working there. I think I had felt some sense of that during my Foundation. There was always an energy around Bradford at the time I went to the art college. It wasn't something that I have really been able to put into words – I am still in touch with Ian Taylor there, and should talk with him about it. In lectures, we were shown performance, happenings, and examples of American land art. I remember one lecture consisted of a performing fire-eater. I now

These images come from negative strips taken
by Goldsworthy in January and March 1977.
The strips record early ephemeral works, which
are interspersed with context and working shots
from around Grove House Farm. They reveal
Goldsworthy's overlapping frames of reference
at that time.

realise that some of the lecturers were directly involved in performance work at that time, of which Albert Hunt was a driving force.

TF: Did a synthesis occur directly between your farm labouring and the work that you began to undertake outside at Lancaster?

AG: It's difficult to recall whether my work was done in reaction to farming, either against it or for it.

TF: In what sense might it have been against?

AG: For some of the reasons I've already mentioned, the industrial side of it; the industrial use or 'misuse'. It has taken me a long time to reconcile myself with farming practices. To some extent I'm still not reconciled with them, but I acknowledge now that farmers are in a front line situation. It is very easy to attack people in the front line. They are producing food, they affect the fields, and they work the land. In that respect, they leave themselves open for criticism in a way that someone who goes to the supermarket does not. Yet they are both doing the same thing, they're both getting food. One takes responsibility for it, one doesn't.

TF: You tell a story about travelling by train from Lancaster, where you had mostly been making geometric-based works outdoors, to Leeds. You talk about observing the landscape from the train window and becoming aware of the field structure as an imposition on the land. Following that journey, you began to undertake works that were more formless, or that tried to reveal rather than impose form. Was that part of your reaction against farming?

AG: Yes, I think it was. The very first works that I did outside were geometric – shapes, lines, squares, cubes made on the beach. I remember at the time not wanting to think about 'shape', so using geometric shapes was a default position. Making a circle or a square means you don't have to think about the shape, it's just there. However, the long line of stones I made at Morecambe Bay sank into the sand. I was interested in the way people reacted to it. The beach was a very social context – people on horses, people walking. The line of stones had to be stepped over; people being confronted by it was more interesting than the shape. I realised that I was actually imposing geometric devices on the landscape. And, yes, there was the experience of going back by train from Lancaster to Leeds. Having spent a few months working on the beach, the geometry and compartmentalisation of the British landscape really struck me: field after field after field, telegraph pole after telegraph pole, the lines connecting them. At that time, I felt a sense of shock that I might be doing the same. I did experience a reaction against the farm system, a system that I recognised was imposed upon the landscape.

TF: However, I think there is a sense in which you wanted to put yourself in that front line. Although you may have wanted to reject the farm 'system', was the relationship of farmer to land, as one that can be fairly unmediated and very palpable, something you perhaps aspired to? Did you want to develop a relationship with the land that was comparable to that which the farmer may have?

Left: Line of stones. Morecambe Bay, Lancashire. April 1976

Right: Squares in sand. Morecambe Bay, Lancashire. March 1976

AG: I think you're right; I wanted a direct connection. As a young artist I felt very confused. I still do, but understand how to live with it. When I was younger I was desperate to find some sort of clarity. I would latch on to one approach; right, I'll make the circles, then swing to the other extreme. When I got off that train, I made a whole series of works without form. They were just about touching. Those extreme swings mark a lot of my very early work.

TF: Physical work was (and is) important to you?

AG: Always. The physical aspect of making stuff, the resistance of it, is vital for me. For me, art cannot exist solely in the mind. It has to be made; it has to come out of some physical process.

TF: You established a rhythm of working very early on that I think is derived from your experience of being on the farm – the immediacy of getting straight into physical work, working in the first light of morning, working in the dark. These are characteristic of your practice, and are a legacy of that time.

Breaking stones. Morecambe Bay, Lancashire. February 1978

AG: The discipline of work is very important. Being able to carry on picking stones, stacking bales, picking potatoes, when every bone in your body is telling you to give up.

TF: It requires stamina.

AG: Yes, stamina has been very important too. Fortunately, I naturally have some stamina. At school I was a cross-country runner, and I would never stop, even at that point in a run where your guts are aching and you have to run through pain. That occurs very often during the making of a sculpture, that moment of 'I'm going to pack in'. There are very few sculptures that don't have that moment, but you learn to run through it.

TF: After finishing college, you didn't continue farm labouring. Nor were you drawn to the farm, or the field, as a context for your practice. You worked up on Ilkley Moor, for instance, or the woods thereabouts – even up until you moved to Brough in the Eden Valley in 1981.

Working on Ilkley Moor, January 1977

AG: When I finished my degree, I planned to go back and live on the farm, in the caravan. My brother John and I were in and out of the system. It was an interesting position to be in. The caravan became my studio too; an environment that I worked in. I had to crawl underneath branches that I'd suspended from the ceiling to get into bed. John was completing an ecology degree at Liverpool Polytechnic and he would come back with ideas. But the farmer died a year before my degree finished. His wife took over the farm, but died six months later. My caravan was auctioned off in the farm sale and my time there ended. After leaving art school I stayed on in Morecambe and carried on working there for a while, before moving to Bentham, on the border between Lancashire and Yorkshire. I was out of employment for several years until I went to Brough, where the Helbeck Estate employed me as a gardener. Moving to Cumbria perhaps marked a renewed interest in the agricultural.

Goldsworthy in the caravan / studio he shared with his brother John at Grove House Farm, April 1976

TF: Yes, and perhaps because of the hill farming context in particular. It is where you first thought about the relationship between open fell and enclosing fold – although it does not emerge in your practice at that point. However, during your period at Brough, you still weren't self-consciously situating your work within the farming, agricultural context were you? If you worked on farmland it tended to be unacknowledged.

AG: To a certain extent, but I was dealing with a different landscape to the one I'd experienced in Yorkshire and Leeds. Cumbria was a mixture of arable, rough field and open fell. It wasn't as intensively farmed.

TF: Perhaps it was through working at Grizedale in 1984 and 1985 that you made those conceptual developments? Is it there that you began to engage with the physical impact that agriculture and farming have upon the land?

AG: Grizedale was set up in 1977 when I was a student at Lancaster, just across the bay from Morecambe. David Nash undertook one of the first residencies there and he came to lecture at the art school. He invited me to go and see him at Grizedale. Even in those early days when I was making only ephemeral work, it represented an opportunity to try out ideas that might become more permanent. Interestingly enough, it was when I went there in 1984 to make Seven Spires, that I really drew on all the practical skills and experiences of working on the farm: how to use a chainsaw, how to use a pulley, how to build things, how to construct on a large scale. Seven Spires was a very physical piece, and it was also done in an industrial forest. Grizedale was an agricultural forest, a plantation, a commercial crop. The pines were grown and cropped, grown and cropped. There was a human relationship to the place that was one of taking and growing. I could engage with that in a way that I probably wouldn't have felt comfortable with if it had been an old wood.

TF: But you used surplus wood which had no economic value, didn't you?

AG: I used windfallen trees for the Spires, even though I was working in a place where the trees were harvested. Partly because that was the way it was at Grizedale in those days, the art wasn't given the status of being allowed to have good wood: you had to use crap wood, but I liked that. So we went searching all over the forest for windfallen trees and we dragged them out manually with ropes. The next work that I made there was a result of looking for straight trees. Oddly, I kept seeing curved trunks that I didn't want for the Spires but it set me off thinking how I might use them: Sidewinder used those curved branches. I went for them because they have no commercial value: foresters would typically cut them out and leave them for firewood. I've always wanted to work with those things that are marginalised, not liked, not wanted – excess.

This page: Building Seven Spires and Sidewinder at Grizedale in 1984 and 1985. Goldsworthy was assisted by John Goldsworthy (far right), Richard Todd, John Ogden, Judith Goldsworthy and several others.

Opposite: Seven Spires. Grizedale, Cumbria. 1984

TF: What about the issue of land access? You have suggested that it was partly the motivation for your move from Brough to Scotland in 1985. Did it become an issue for you at Brough?

AG: I love the idea of North and of living in the North. It is a very important notion to me. However, one of the attractions of coming to Scotland was access to the land. In England at that time, as I experienced it, there was always a tension attached to access.

TF: To farmland?

AG: Yes, and I knew about those tensions from the other side: how the farmers felt about people walking through their land. I remember working in a quarry above Brough. I walked out into a shooting party, and I was quickly rounded on by the landowner. I was caught, but doing what? Walking on a bit of ground, making a work. It's not as simple as I'm making it sound. I usually ask a farmer's permission to make work in their woods and fields. Going to a farmer and saying 'I'm an artist, I make art in the landscape, then photograph it, and I want to work in your wood, is that okay?', is quite tough, but I would always do that, even when I came to Scotland. Right of access doesn't give you the right to make sculpture in someone's field. Brough was probably where I became more aware of the social nature of the landscape. The making of work in a place you don't own makes you think differently. Even now, I prefer to work on other people's land. It puts me in a different position. I came to Scotland because of right of access. In the mid-1980s that had a huge effect on the way I looked at the landscape and the way I dealt with farmers. My art really opened up to the greater landscape when I moved to Penpont, in a way it had never before been able to. It is when I began working with the fields. That was a direct result of the attitude of the people here. If I don't feel right in a place the work can become tiny and hidden.

TF: When you arrived in Penpont you leased some land from the Buccleuch Estates as an 'outdoor studio'. The plot encompasses about three acres and you called it Stone Wood. Can you talk about why you wanted to lease the land? You were familiar with David Nash's Cae'n-y-Coed plantings in north Wales. Were you interested in some of those ideas?

AG: Yes, I'd seen David's piece of ground and I'm sure I recognised it as something I would be interested in doing. The local arts officer, Jenny Wilson, introduced herself to me and she subsequently introduced me to the Earl of Dalkeith. I came to Penpont primarily because of the need for a studio, which I found in the form of an old granary in the middle of the village. I managed to buy it with the financial support of the Fabian Carlsson Gallery. It was a time to experiment with studios – both inside and out. The Buccleuch Estates asked me to identify land that I would be interested in leasing. What became known as Stone Wood was the very first place that I worked in when I came to Penpont. It was about six acres – part wood and part field – the rough ground where farmers fed their animals in winter to avoid damage to good fields. It was also where the wood turned to field. I never knew at that time whether the wood was turning to field or the field was becoming wood. In these circumstances, a wood usually becomes smaller, and I was attracted to the idea of securing it. I asked for the whole field and, farmers being farmers, I didn't get it. They have to negotiate, so I got half a field. The whole process that went on, with the farmer and the landowner, was interesting to me. There was dialogue because of this exchange of land. As a result of the division, I had to build a wall to divide the field and mark the new boundary. Building a wall was quite expensive. Common Ground helped me raise funds in the form of sponsorship – people gave me money in exchange for work that was made from the land for the next few years. The Give and Take Wall has two enclosures in it, and forms the shape of an 's'. The opening to one enclosure is on my land, but the actual chamber that I enter is on the farmer's land, and his entrance opens out into a fold which is on mine. So it's a 'give and take' wall – it's about the exchange that took place.

TF: Did the farmer simply accept what you proposed for the division?

AG: I can't remember there being any huge opposition. The farmer is someone whom I've got to know quite well since. He and his family have been very supportive; I worked on their fields too and in a small slate quarry on their farm. It's very rare for the permanent works to arrive at the final idea immediately: there are always many permutations.

TF: This was the first work where you were using agricultural spaces, processes and forms directly?

AG: It was a dry stone wall, a line and two circular forms; geometric shapes that had come out of agricultural forms already present in the landscape. The folds in this area are beautifully made and usually circular. Some sit in unusually striking positions. Two in particular seem to have been placed with some aesthetic judgement – one on the Dalveen Pass and one on the Mennock Pass. They are such beautiful objects and represented a reconciliation with geometric shape, allowing me to work with it in a way that had meaning.

TF: Consistent with the creation of the **Give and Take Wall**, which
you built with Joe Smith, you were invited by Dick Capel to go to the
Yorkshire Dales National Park, and you proposed another 'wall work'
for Mossdale Farm, which was then rejected. That was the first time
you proposed the wall as sculpture?

AG: When I made the Give and Take Wall, I also had ideas for
sculptures which might exist inside the folds, but that was soon put to
one side. It was really the space that became the sculpture. That, and
the change that occurred to the land because of the wall being there.
With Mossdale Farm, I can't quite remember if there was an existing
wall or not, or whether I was going to rebuild one. The Give and Take
Wall released a number of works that didn't have the same meaning
or connection to space as that first one did. One work I proposed for
the south of France included two circular wall structures that had no
reference to walls that already existed there; they were simply
geometric shapes.

TF: So in a sense the validity of the wall is connected to the notion of
the system you talked about earlier?

Opposite:
Give and Take Wall
Stone Wood, Scaur Glen
1988
Photographed shortly after completion.

This page: proposal drawing for
Mossdale Farm, Yorkshire. 1988-89

AG: In Britain, a circular wall or an enclosure is first seen as a farming structure. In the south of France it's seen as a sculpture. There is something subversive about making an agricultural enclosure as an artwork.

TF: Do you feel those folds that are more or less spatial devices, or 'rooms' as you often refer to them, to be less successful than those that are specific to a certain context?

AG: They can work, and they have been successful when I have made them; Room, which I made at Kentuck Knob in Pennsylvania for instance, or Ile de Vassivière, where I made two joined folds. However, I feel far more comfortable and interested in those that are made in a place where there are, or have been, existing folds or walls. When I reprised the Mossdale proposal at Grizedale, it did respond to the line of an existing old boundary wall that was 'redrawn' by my work. For me it gave the work strength in a similar way that the exchange of land at Stone Wood gave strength to the Give and Take Wall

Left: Two Folds.
Ile de Vassivière, Limousin. 1992

Below: Room. Kentuck Knob, Pennsylvania. 1992

They both had a meaning beyond being an aesthetically pleasing shape in the landscape – both are rooted in the place. That made me start thinking of what had gone before – or the history of place – in a way that I don't think I had previously.

TF: The **Wall that went for a walk** is certainly one of your first major commissions to reference layers of land use. You talk about being aware that Grizedale was once fields, about the wall being evidence of that and the exclusion of sheep and grazing farming, and the subsequent use of the land for timber farming. You reveal an awareness of the cyclical use of the land on a large scale.

AG: Recently I walked up to a vantage point looking down on the Give and Take Wall that I last went to when I completed the wall to photograph it. Seeing it from above made me see its context and I realised how it connected to the walls around it, which were like veins running through the landscape. I'd tapped into something bigger than just my work. That gave me a real sense of continuation of something that already existed in the landscape.

TF: Whilst working on the wall at Grizedale in 1990 you wrote, 'I don't expect that this sculpture will stay the same because the environment

Give and Take Wall
Stone Wood, Scaur Glen
1988

Give and Take Wall
Stone Wood, Scaur Glen
1988

Photographed in 1993 and 2006

won't stay the same, and this landscape will change – it could be felled, and if it is, what sense will my sculpture then make?'. You had a sense of the changes that can be witnessed even within a generation. From the **Wall that went for a walk**, you then made a series of wall works in New England on the east coast of the USA. You shifted from an essentially agricultural context, from Cumbria, to one that is effectively now post-agricultural. New England and Cumbria are two contexts historically linked through the occurrence of an agricultural diaspora. Did you feel a conceptual connection between Cumbria and New England, or something more dissonant?

AG: Much of the land around where I live in Scotland, and indeed the land in Cumbria upon which sheepfolds are typically sited, is marginal ground. Although the Sheepfolds Project across Cumbria is a celebration, an acknowledgement of the richness that farmers can bring to the landscape, it is also about change. Those folds in which I have worked are often empty vessels. They no longer have any purpose, any direction. I am also aware that the future of hill farming is very precarious. And you can see that happening at Stone Wood: the Give and Take Wall has prevented sheep from encroaching on to my side, and consequently, it is now overgrown with trees – the absence of sheep has allowed the wood to regenerate. Going to New England and seeing how the field systems have given way to completely wooded ground perhaps is a view of what Britain could look like in the future. That brings with it a sense of precariousness, for the lives and livelihoods of hill farmers in particular.

Wall that went for a walk
Grizedale, Cumbria
1990

TF: When you were invited to make that first proposal for New York State, in the first instance you encountered a very densely reforested area. Did you feel a sense of distinction between Grizedale, parts of which are reforested and farmed, and occasionally clear-felled, and this new area that you were working in? It was at one point agricultural but simply because of the discontinuation of that practice it has reforested naturally.

AG: It's difficult to say when the full implications of a place become apparent. It doesn't happen immediately. The old walls of New England were interesting because I had been primed by Grizedale. When the early settlers went there from places like Cumbria, they cleared and felled the woods to make fields and farms. The ground was very stony so they made walls out of the stone, all of which created visual connections to the British landscape. The full significance of being in a wood that was once fields occurred over a longer period of time. The first commissioned work I made in New England, Wood Through Wall, drew out some of the concerns of Grizedale – the trees and the wall. I rebuilt a length of wall in a wooded area, and embedded a tree horizontally within it. When I found the derelict wall, traces of a 'cut' were still visible, perhaps where a gate would have been positioned. When we rebuilt the wall I kept the 'cut', so the tree appears as if it is cut by the entrance.

TF: You very quickly established a conceptual grounding in the New England context.

AG: It was a place where I could continue things that I'd unearthed at Grizedale. There is always a tension between tree and wall. Trees eventually brought down parts of the Grizedale wall. The tension is evocative of the historical tension between a forested and a farmed landscape. A field, cleared of trees, is the site of a battle that has occurred between a farmer and the land. It is the forum in which considerable hardship has occurred to turn wooded land into a productive field. I've been in reforested areas thick with briars and thorns; they are abrasive places, not easy to walk through. You get a powerful sense of the struggle of clearing that wood, but also the power of growth to regenerate and reclaim that field. Coming back to Britain, seeing the open fields that I had to some extent taken for granted, made me realise how quickly those fields would revert back to woodland if no longer farmed. Fields and treeless mountains are there only because of the activities of farming. The walls I've made in Britain are part of a still vigorous farming practice. Walling is a very effective way of dividing a field. I like the contemporary nature of this practice, which is absent in the USA, at least in an agricultural form, and which therefore changes the context and meaning of the work.

Opposite: Wood Through Wall. Westchester County, New York. 1993
Below: Storm King Wall. Mountainville, New York. 1997-1999

TF: You continued to develop those conceptual connections or 'tensions' over the next few years. The connection between Cumbria, the southwest of Scotland, and New England remained strong for you and you seemed to work alternately between them. For instance, in 1995, you were invited to make a proposal for a work at Storm King in Mountainville, New York, which you then built over the period 1997-1999. Parallel with that, you were developing the **Sheepfolds Project**, with Steve Chettle, commissioned by Cumbria County Council. At Storm King you were working in a landscape that had recovered itself from intensive farming, but in Cumbria you were working where large areas continue to rely on the agricultural economy. Yet, as would become apparent through the **Sheepfolds Project**, the idea of an agricultural / post-agricultural binary seems somewhat simplistic. Cumbria proved to be a complex context: the ubiquitous sheepfold structures, or at least their traces, allowed you to consider the contemporary agricultural situation which is itself subject to encroaching urbanisation.

AG: Folds are identifiable agricultural spaces – rooms in which farmers work. The majority are no longer used. They seemed interesting spaces in which to put work that would connect with their agricultural use. In a broader way this places my touch where others have already been – the layering of human activity. Folds are also interesting to walk into – I was drawn to the tension of entering that space, enclosed and intimate, after being on the open fell. I enjoy the way that people will look in, half expecting to see a sheep bolt. So there is a release of energy. In placing a rock inside, there is a moment when the rock is seen as something alive. I have always tried to see stone as something alive. I had hoped that the Sheepfolds Project would cover all areas of Cumbria, and occur in urban as well as agricultural spaces. I made urban proposals, for instance, one for Carlisle Civic Centre. According to one of the historic maps, the Civic Centre stands in the vicinity of where an old fold once stood. I wanted to make the fold inside the Civic Centre offices, as a temporary work, possibly straddling rooms inside the building, connecting one room to another. People would have had to walk round the stone structure – it would have been interesting to see how they dealt with it inside an office space; a reminder of what was once there, as well as a connection between inside and out. However, urban folds proved somewhat difficult to achieve – Carlisle City Council refused two proposals for the Civic Centre, and only at the very end of the project will I manage to make an urban fold at Wigton; and only because of the persistence of their town council. It is on the site of an old fold which no longer exists, and will be on the corner of a crossroads. There are street signs and an electricity box that are positioned at the perimeter of the site and services that run through it. It also adjoins a petrol station. There are issues of road visibility. I have struggled for a long time with this fold. In the end I will make a fold, the height and shape of which will be determined by the restrictions imposed by urban regulations. The street signs will be incorporated into the wall. The fold will be a reminder of what was there before, but it will also talk about how that space has changed.

Wigton Pinfold site shot, February 1997

TF: The **Sheepfolds Project** is probably the first time in a public context you consciously sought the opinion – the permission – of farmers, or even their creative engagement, and certainly their tolerance. You drew the farmer quite directly into the conceptual and administrative process of your project. With all the folds, you had to approach landowners, commoners, parish councils, and others. A huge number of elements came into play insofar as you talk about the landscape being social. You had all these groups suddenly mediating the possible existence of a sculpture. The appearance or non-appearance of a fold or work was determined by these parties. Did that experience feel frustrating or were you comfortable with it? Is it sometimes successful, sometimes less so?

AG: All of those things. But I have always had to deal with landowners and farmers. As we discussed earlier, my relationship with landowners affects where I can work, and to some extent, what I can make. If they were open-minded, the work might be bigger. If they really didn't want me around then I would sneak in and make something small. It has made my work more resilient and unpredictable. That there are only fifty or so folds made out of the intended one hundred is very much in keeping with the spirit of the Sheepfolds Project. I didn't know what the end results would be, and it was a very organic process as to where a fold would be made. Whether, and indeed where, a fold could be made was determined not just by me, but also by the people who owned the fold, or the land on which it stood. Not only did they have to grant me permission to make it, but they also had to grant public access to it as well. At times it was incredibly disappointing, putting in huge amounts of effort to make a work in a place, only to be refused.

TF: So it required pragmatism?

AG: Pragmatism, yes. However, the notion and implications of something being refused became a theme of the project too. Hearing that you can't make something doesn't mean that idea goes away. I was refused permission to make a cone inside one particular fold at

Winton. That fold was personally very important for me, as it was one of the first folds that I encountered when living at Brough.

TF: You've talked about that particular fold as being at the bottom of various fells, and of its seeming to be a nucleus, a basis or nub.

AG: It was. The surrounding fields become smaller and smaller as they reach this central collection area, in which there is a circular fold. It feels like the heart of the landscape. It was instrumental as it showed me how the fold can become a focus of its surroundings. I really wanted to acknowledge that fold in the Project, and I talked for several hours to village representatives, but was still refused permission.

Top: Stone 13. Drove Stone Folds. Casterton, Cumbria. 1996
Bottom: Stone 16. Drove Stone Folds. Casterton, Cumbria. 1996

TF: Why do you think they refused?

AG: There are a number of possible reasons. But those were the very reasons I wanted to make the Project in Cumbria: to confront that attitude that the landscape is something unchanging and fixed. At a meeting for another fold a couple of miles away in Hartley – another refusal – someone said 'this landscape is antique and you don't put a new thing in something that is antique'. The landscape is very old, but it is not an antique, it is not dead, not finished. There are things that are new and there are things that are old; there are things that are dead and things that are born. The notion of new things in Cumbria is a very difficult one for some people: they want everything to look as though it's always been there.

TF: But you're not bringing a new structure into the Cumbrian landscape. You are working with existing structures, or with the footings of those once present. On the one hand the fold feels like an historical constant in the landscape. However, its fortunes as a useful structure, and its various permutations, have been determined by agricultural and cultural shifts and patterns. Perhaps that tension manifested with some communities?

AG: Whilst my folds make strong connections to forms and materials that are in the landscape, they are nonetheless very contemporary works. I suppose some people found that difficult, alongside a lot of bloody-mindedness about the Project being a waste of money. Walls have always been repaired – gapped. Rebuilding is part of their life. Left alone they will collapse over time through the rubbing of animals, settlement, crumbling stone. There are miles of derelict walls that will never be rebuilt, just as there are miles of good standing walls. The precedent of wall repair allows me the opportunity to engage with the old structure. I guess the issue is – do I build a fold in the same way that it was originally, even though there is no agricultural need or use for that fold, or do I rebuild it in what I feel was the spirit in which it was first made and find a new purpose for it being made? The needs of a sculpture for me are real, important and practical, if it is to work. As a sculptor I need the fold to work in, as a farmer once needed it for his sheep. The Sheepfolds Project is rooted in different, but still practical needs. The results, I hope, are folds with a purpose.

TF: There is a strong conceptual element to the **Sheepfolds Project**. Perhaps that was problematic for some? You were inviting people to engage in a conceptual process about their environment.

AG: The Project went through a very low period not far into it, after the initial phase in 1996/1997, and the completion of Drove Stones at Casterton. It felt as though Cumbria was caught off guard. It confused people. At first there was an acceptance – we were building sheepfolds, and how can someone not want us to do that? Once it became more widely known that it was an 'art project' resistance built up, particularly in the Eden Valley and around Brough where I used to live. Several folds were, consequently, refused. Not that the Project did not have supporters: at that same meeting at Hartley, a teacher in a local school said that this was a chance to put something back. Ultimately the Project ground to a halt for a few years before we resumed and, when it did reappear, it was at the invitation of Brough Primary School and Bolton Parish Council. For me it is curious and unexpected that to rebuild a sheepfold has now become one of those things you do to celebrate heritage events, like planting a tree.

TF: Returning to Storm King in New York State, to make the **Storm King Wall**, you shifted from fold to wall again. What is the difference between fold and wall for you? Storm King must have felt considerably more protected as a working context.

AG: There is a difference between a wall and a fold. The fold is an enclosed space, like a microcosm of the field. The Storm King Wall isn't an enclosed space: it is a line, it draws space – draws the place wherein it's made. Drawing is a good word to describe many aspects of the making of a wall. The stone is drawn out of the ground; it is drawn to the place. In the case of Mountjoy Farm in Cumbria, where two large stones were dragged through fields to the folds, they drew the landscape in the process, and left a muddy trail. The wall also draws from the past, especially when made on the line of an old wall. The Storm King Wall is a line that divides wood from field – it is about that same tension between tree and wood. Originally the wall was made after the wood was cleared, and then seeds found haven alongside the wall where they were untouched by the plough and grew, eventually causing the wall to collapse. My wall was a reconciliation between wall and tree, in that the wall goes around the trees rather than cutting them down. Although I was dealing with the same concerns of a social landscape, Storm King offered a far more protected space than Cumbria. I loved working there, it was fantastic to work with that level of support and care, and the Wall is being looked after so thoughtfully. I like it for that, but it is a comfortable place to work in, compared to Cumbria; it is important that I keep my feet in regular, working agricultural communities and landscapes.

Left: South Fold. Mountjoy Farm Tree Folds. Underbarrow, Cumbria. 2000–2001
Right: Mud tracks left by boulder as it slid down the hillside at Mountjoy Farm on 5 December 2000

TF: Through 1997 you worked on projects in both Cumbria and New England. In June, you undertook the **Drove Arch** project – part of the **Sheepfolds Project**. For that, you assembled the same small red sandstone arch at various fold sites situated along the route of the old A6. Your trajectory with the **Drove Arch** was to follow the traditional drove route, travelling from Scotland through Cumbria to north Yorkshire. You were also developing the **Storm King Wall** at that time. Both of these works rely on and reference economically determined movement in agriculture, be it of livestock or of people. The structures that you utilise are evidence or accretions of that movement. This is something that I think you have drawn out through your work on various levels. Can you talk about **Drove Arch**, and the concept of movement and agricultural shift as it bears upon your work?

AG: Yes, perhaps it struck me when I first saw the Give and Take Wall from that high vantage point, seeing the work that I had made connected into this pre-existing network of roads, walls and lines. Drove roads are the old routes along which livestock, usually sheep and cattle, were taken to market, often ultimately leading to London. Reference to them is still very evident in the names of roads.

TF: So drove routes were economic routes?

AG: They were, and they were the connections between agriculture and the city. I was interested in that link. It was also important that some aspect of the Sheepfolds Project began outside Cumbria, went through Cumbria, and ended up out of Cumbria. I wanted to incorporate a sense of things that passed through a place, and their effect on other places.

TF: Are you talking about a sense of flow through the land?

AG: Yes, things flow through the landscape – like the economic river of animals. Then there is the human flow. People have to leave the place in which they have lived, often for generations, because of a shift in economic circumstances. Historically there have been huge displacements because of agriculture. Sheep have been at the centre of a lot of those changes and have had a powerful impact on the country. Abbeys, monasteries and towns were built on the wool trade. The economic importance of wool and sheep took precedence when it came to Inclosure Acts in England and the Clearances in Scotland. Sheep are often perceived as being a pastoral, cute, benevolent feature of the landscape. Actually they have had an enormous impact on the land, socially, politically and environmentally. I wanted the Sheepfolds Project to bring out some of that effect.

TF: The **Drove Arch** project had a kind of cumulative effect, didn't it?

AG: I wanted to connect one fold to another along the route, using identifiable spaces. Animals were driven along the drove route. They would have had to stop overnight, and there were enclosures along the route that were possibly places where animals were kept. I took a small red sandstone arch from Scotland and built and rebuilt it in folds along the route. Sometimes the arch was made because I wanted to make it in a place that looked interesting, like between two rocks, underneath some arches, in or alongside a building, or in the middle of a road. The arch made in the middle of the road was one of the strongest.

Drove Arch. Greenholme Show, Cumbria. 14 July 1997

TF: Did anyone want to drive around it?

AG: No, but the chance that someone could come was always there. I had previously built an arch at the side of the road, but I thought, 'no, I've got to build it in the middle of the road'. On this occasion, I noticed a country lane along the drove route that wasn't used too much, and I got up very early in the morning to make it: a stone arch in the middle of the road.

TF: Were some of the folds along that route difficult to locate? Had parts changed significantly?

AG: We were quite looking forward to places that had significantly changed and I think the one that comes to mind was by Armstrong's, a haulage company at Longtown. There was no fold there, but we knew there was a fold on the map. It was alongside the company car park, which was an interesting place to find myself in. Many of the others were just there alongside the roads and somewhat derelict.

TF: We have mentioned that after the **Sheepfolds Project**, the farmed landscape became much more of a presence in your ephemeral work. You began to use wool around 1996, and in 1997/1998 you produced a series of what you call **Sheep Paintings**. Can you talk about those?

Drove Arch. Old Scotch Road, Cumbria. 16-17 June 1997

AG: The Sheepfolds Project, and perhaps the Coleridge's Walk series that I did as part of it, drew me to materials that I had not worked with – wool in particular. Not to use wool or sheep would be a real omission. Yet I realise it is a very difficult material to work with, for all the obvious reasons.

TF: Can you describe the **Coleridge's Walk** series?

AG: I always wanted the Sheepfolds Project to have an ephemeral element. One of the ways to give that a structure was to follow the line of the walk that Samuel Taylor Coleridge made through the Lakes. One of the reasons to work with existing places or routes is that I'm not dictating entirely what this structure is going to be. I wanted to be forced into responding to places. I learned that Coleridge made a walk done just for it's own sake – a nine-day circular walk around the Lake District. Why did he do the walk? I am not sure – perhaps to recover from his drug addiction. I did not make my walk as a homage; it was more to have an identifiable line to follow, to acknowledge that when we walk, particularly in the British landscape, we are walking on paths where people have been before. This connects us to the human presence in places. I chose to follow Coleridge's route, being mindful of that, rather than aligning myself with a pastoral tradition. I have always found problems with words such as 'Romantic' or 'pastoral' when applied to my work.

TF: So during the **Sheepfolds Project** you used new materials – wool for instance.

AG: Wool and walls became much, much more interesting as subject matter. As did the field, and the presence of the farmer.

TF: The presence of the farmer; in what way?

AG: Well, insofar as the field is a field because of the farmer's work. When you work with a field, you are working with what the farmer does, with the impact of it. I often make work in the tracks made by tractors or trailers. There is also the way farmers feed their animals – often they put hay into containers, or put salt licks out into the field. I noticed that these then had to be moved because the ground around them gets very muddy.

Andrew Morton, neighbouring farmer and friend of Goldsworthy's, approaching and driving through a small work. Morton suggested he should drive round. Goldsworthy declined his offer and recorded the demise of the work. 8 March 2005

TF: This led to your **Sheep Painting** series?

AG: I noticed that the containers left geometric shapes amongst an explosion of mud, which I felt was visually very powerful. I decided to work with this by laying canvases out in the field and placing food containers or salt licks on them. The sheep walked over the canvas to get to the salt, and left traces. After a while we moved the canvas, took the container off and had what appeared to be formal abstract paintings when stretched on the wall. But they are a way of thinking about the impact of the farmers' work, how they sculpt and paint the landscape. I think the Sheep Paintings show something of the grittier side of agriculture. Working with wool, to get back to that, has been a tough thing to do. I have a technical desire to get a 'line' of the wool, and take the wooliness out of the material, to make it taut. It is particularly difficult to make wool work that is tight and incisive. In one of my most successful early attempts I stretched wool along the top of a dry stone wall – 'drawing' the wall, and the places in which it had collapsed. The previous winter I had done a similar line on the same wall in snow. The wall was a line drawn between fields to contain sheep. Over time the wall had become broken, partially because of the erosive effect of winter and sheep jumping over it. I felt it was in the spirit of the place to draw the wall first with snow and then with wool. More recent works with wool have been made on river rocks. I am sure that finding washfolds – folds alongside streams where sheep were gathered before being thrown into the water – drew my attention to the connection between wool and water. Dipping wool in water not only makes it whiter, it also allows me to extract a far tighter line than when the wool is dry. The taut energy in these works is for me a way of trying to understand the tension that has always existed between farm, sheep and the land.

TF: The outbreak of Foot and Mouth Disease in 2001 affected the second phase of the **Sheepfolds Project**, effectively suspending it for eight or nine months, so you had to retreat into your studio. Can you talk about that experience and perhaps how it precipitated a personal sense of enclosure for you, and how you developed ways of working

AG: The boundary of my own garden, my own property, was the limit of where I could work. It was a very difficult time. The disease was prevalent in Dumfriesshire; the white line on the road that runs through Penpont determined where the D notice was. We were right on the edge, where animals could not be moved at all. So in fact the farmer who has the land around my house could bring sheep here, but he couldn't take them back because one way was on the right side of the road and one wasn't. It was a very restricted time and some of those lines seemed so arbitrary. The fact that I could go up to the fence and work, but couldn't go into the field…the white line on the middle of the road…these lines took on so much significance at that time. I did a series of burnt wool pieces. It felt like the landscape was being burnt off. Obviously there were fires, there was the smell, and the whole atmosphere was very strange. I had to deal with that, so I worked on my boundary. A lot of the work was made about that boundary, the fence line. I worked on and up to the fence; I made lines that went up to it, but that couldn't go beyond. Restriction and access were always part of the Sheepfolds Project. There was an element of 'you can't make a work there, you can't walk here, you can't do that there', factors that were balanced by the invitations to work.

Wool stretched
across front of gate
held with thorns
Penpont, Dumfriesshire
May 2001

Burning wool
Penpont, Dumfriesshire
May 2001

TF: Can I ask about the film **Rivers and Tides**, in particular the segment that focuses on shots of cattle and sheep, and perhaps refer back to some of the points you made about following the line of Coleridge's walk? I felt that this particular sequence of the film reinforced a pastoral view of your work, or certainly constructed a very simplified reading of the agricultural context in which you work. It struck me less as a perception of the British landscape from the point of view of those who work it, than as an external perception looking in. How do you feel about that?

AG: I felt it presented an urban view of the landscape as something that is pastoral. Landscape is beautiful to look at, but as anybody who works with animals, on a farm, or with the land knows, it is also raw and harsh. I think that my art has suffered from the same misreading. The land, for many, is a pastoral backdrop to the weekend, an antidote to the nitty-gritty of the urban life – the 'real' life. Obviously when you work outside and live in the countryside, it is not a pastoral retreat. Ultimately, it is a place where life, death, and decay occur in a potent and powerful way. It is the toughest place to work as far as I'm concerned. It is not some sort of idyll – it is often physically and psychologically uncomfortable and is at times severe and disturbing. I cannot walk far from my house without coming across something dying and decaying. There is also a powerful sense of change and growth. I sometimes wonder if regulations that now require farmers to remove dead animals immediately have more to do with the unpleasantness of seeing a decaying carcass than any health issues – especially when an animal dies way out on the fell where it would have become food for other animals. There are even regulations now that restrict the winter feeding of stock to avoid the mess that occurs when animals gather in one place. Farmers try to feed animals in one place to contain the damage to one area. There are probably good reasons in some places for this to be regulated, but I wonder if this is again being driven by a wish to conceal what some people consider unpleasant to look at. Dead animals and the shit around feeding places are difficult subject matter, but I have managed to make some work with both that I hope isn't gratuitous or sensationalist.

TF: But what about the way you frame your work photographically? Very rarely in your photography do you consciously acknowledge the farmed landscape, particularly those aspects that you have just spoken about. Nor do you necessarily acknowledge the farmed field as a 'frame' in itself. Mostly you frame your work in a very iconic way. I know that you do present 'context' shots of your work alongside the more frontal, centrally framed shots. For me, the former are always the more interesting, where your work appears almost incidental. Do you think there is a tension between how you have photographed and presented your ephemeral work, and your increased awareness of the field/landscape as a forum for your work? When you photograph your work, don't you isolate it from that forum?

AG: I think there is a problem here. There has always been a tension between the photograph and the context: not just the context, but also the work being outdoors. It has been difficult not to elevate the photograph: it is a result of the ways I work, it is not the reason. I feel that within its limitations the photograph should try to show the work for what it is.

TF: But most people don't have access to a large proportion of your work, and the way that it is communicated to them privileges particular views of it, often centrally framed. I think the fact that you use a square format for a lot of your photography helps to achieve that view of your ephemeral work. People typically experience your ephemeral work in a way that I feel extracts it from the total context in which you worked. Having observed you at work, you do work with a 'total context'. From 1996 onwards, you began to use a panoramic camera and there is, I think, a correlation between that new, wider format and the inclusion of fields within the frame.

AG: The square format presents the work in a simple fashion. It has no hierarchy. I don't want to take unusual angles and I don't want to use things that might act as additional interpretation of the work. Nonetheless, when I pick up the camera and frame the work, I am making decisions about how it looks, and that is usually determined by being as simple and straightforward as possible. The only way that I could possibly show a place more completely might be through film. Until recently, I have resisted film just because I have felt that documentation has to be kept within bounds. At the moment I am thinking of doing some video works, particularly documenting the Rainshadows as moving images. There has always been a tension between the sculpture and the photograph. It is a tension that I live with, and at times it has been a creative one.

TF: Can we talk about Digne-Les-Bains, and the **Refuges d'Art** project that you are developing there with the Musée Gassendi and the Réserve Géologique de Haute-Provence? Like the **Sheepfolds Project**, it is a large-scale project that is developing rather organically over time. There are other correspondences between the two: for instance, where the **Sheepfolds Project** draws on shifts that occurred in Cumbria between fell and valley, and between village and town, a similar set of concerns underpins the **Refuges d'Art** project, does it not?

AG: Yes, there are similarities there. I worked on Sheepfolds for ten years, and through that process learned a lot about the social nature and structure of the land, the people, the past, and how to draw those things into the works. The Sheepfolds Project was perhaps a laboratory, which hugely benefited the works made in Digne. There is also a sense of progression, a development. Ideas first touched on in the Sheepfolds Project have manifested themselves in a much stronger fashion in Digne: it is more grounded, rooted, and connected to the social landscape and the people who now live there. It is conceptually more robust.

TF: Can you describe the **Refuges d'Art** project?

AG: It draws on the strongest elements of the Sheepfolds Project – the connections that run through a place. That is very important. I am not just making objects, I am making a link, a vein that runs through it. The Drove Arch was an attempt to do that in Cumbria. The Drove Stones at Casterton is another group of sculptures where the track that links the folds, and the space between them, is as important as the folds themselves. Fold, then field, fold, and then field: it sets a rhythm in the sculpture that is beyond just the stone of which it is made. It is about the movement of walking, about space, so I have drawn on these ingredients to make a nine-day walk in Digne, originally conceived to link three guardian sculptures that I had already made in three valleys that are overseen by the Réserve Géologique. Guy Martini, then the director, and Nadine Gomez asked me to make those Sentinelles, one in each valley and independent. I then started looking at the huge number of old derelict buildings in which there were such interesting spaces. I began to think if I rebuilt those places, in the rebuilding could I make something which would have a dialogue with those aspects? Would it produce something?

Completion of Sentinelle, Authon. Digne-Les-Bains, France. 2000

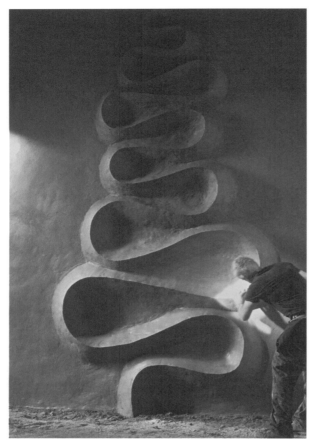

Left:
Completing Refuge d'Art, Esclangon. Digne-Les-Bains, France. 2005

Below:
Construction of Refuge d'Art, Chapelle Sainte-Madeleine. Digne-Les-Bains, France. 2002

Like the Sheepfolds, it was not driven by some nostalgic sense of wanting to restore the landscape. Many of the sheepfolds in Cumbria on top of the hills are used by people for shelter. Guy Martini and I were siting one of the Sentinelles and we began to think, can we walk from this one to that one? He went back to look at old maps, and found that not only could one walk there, but that the routes are old roads – packhorse routes that joined mountain top villages. Now we drive around, but then the quickest way of travel was over the hill. Not only were there roads, there were abandoned villages, churches on top of the mountains. So there was this incredible history of people living here, and it seemed a beautiful opportunity to make a work that was about human presence in the landscape, and to make a walk that would connect the sculptures, which would become a work in its own right. It would go on top of the mountains and drop down into villages, so that you shift between populated and unpopulated places. The rebuilt houses and barns would become refuges where people could sleep, not just shelter, but actually live with the sculpture for a while. Not all of the houses are places to sleep in, but many will be. That idea of being part of a work is so profoundly different to just going and staying with it for a few minutes, or an hour. This particular aspect has made the Refuges d'Art project far more meaningful for me. I couldn't have reached that level of understanding without the Sheepfolds Project. Equally as important, perhaps, is that out of the planned one hundred sheepfolds, only fifty or so were made, so I had to be adaptable. If a particular proposal wasn't permitted, I shifted to another area, another place. The Sheepfolds Project has reached a conclusion in my mind. When the Wigton Pinfold is complete, I'll probably have done as much as I want to do with the particular project. I now see far more potential in Digne to take these ideas forward, and to stretch myself. Digne itself is becoming a laboratory for other works in other places. It's had a huge impact on my subsequent commissions elsewhere.

TF: The idea of the house as a protective enclosure, or a 'refuge', actually has its roots in the **Sheepfolds Project**, doesn't it? Specifically with Casterton. On Fellfoot Road, one of the small square folds had actually been a barn or a shepherd's hut.

AG: It was already derelict, but the remains of it were there. In my diaries, at that time, I said how great it would be actually to put a stone in this place, and rebuild the barn.

TF: Is that something you eventually did?

AG: At that time there was a desire to keep the Drove Stones conceptually tight, and to keep the uniformity. It would have been an anomaly to have had a barn in there, and also there weren't the finances to rebuild the hut. It was not possible, just not possible. It was a shock to look back in my diaries recently and see that.

TF: In Digne, the route will be open to walkers as a nine-day walk. It will obviously bring some kind of economic benefits. Is this part of your thinking?

AG: I live in a rural place and I identify strongly with the problems of rural places; the economic situation can be pretty dire. Young people don't have jobs and it's hard to make a living. So, yes, that is an important side of the project. Digne is quite a forward-thinking, small town, trying to make itself viable in all sorts of ways – the Réserve Géologique is an astonishing institution to have set up there. It's something very specific, not a theme park, not superficial. It encourages people to come for a precise reason, and that's attractive. There's more of an engagement with the place if you go there for the geology, or you go there walking by yourself on the hills. What I perceive as being potentially problematic is the move towards 'drive-in' nature. Lay-bys with a sign. You look at the landscape and get back in your car. Very reminiscent of when I first went to the USA as an eleven year old. I'll never forget going round some of the National Parks, particularly the Painted Desert. Getting in a car, getting out, taking a picture, getting back in. For me, this is not the way to engage with landscape. So, I realised that the Sentinelles, which were purposely made as journey guardians, were nonetheless alongside roads, which fell into this 'drive-through, drive-in, look at, move on' impulse. I felt it needed a counter-point, something different that would bring people to walk the hills rather than drive. They would have to stay in villages and contribute economically to the area. The Reserve employs people with whom I've worked very closely, who will act as guides to visitors, and that brings economic benefits too. But more than that, there is a wonderful exchange that occurs between the walker and the people of the place, and the guides. There is a social dialogue with someone who lives there, knows and breathes the place. So all of these things are part and parcel of the idea. The Refuges d'Art project had its challenges, suffered huge resistance from some people. Where works occur, very vigorous discussions take place that I like – I don't particularly enjoy being attacked, but it's good for me and makes the project stronger.

TF: In many of your commissioned works, you interweave references to the geological and the agricultural. You do this through the use of glacial boulders or glacial rubble which, ploughed from the fields, becomes walling stone. Obviously, Digne is an area of geological significance, but it is also a literal interface between the human working of the land and geological bedrock. Can you talk about how you relate the geological and agricultural, the land as a geological deposit and as an agricultured context?

AG: I think I've tried to see the forces of change in agriculture in a geological way. Take Drove Stones at Casterton: when you first see those stones in the folds, you think 'you shouldn't move big stones, they 'belong' in the place they stand'. Then you look a little deeper, and realise that actually they don't 'belong' there. They were brought by glaciers from a long way away. Then you look at the walls and you see they have been drawn out of the fields through the process of farming. The movement of stone, which initially occurred glacially is being continued by farmers – pulling off the stones, and rolling them from the field. Boulders in fields are often left because they are too big to be moved by farmers. So with Drove Stones, I felt it was very much in the spirit of the material and the place, both geologically and agriculturally, to move stones and to put them into walls

TF: For you, the agricultural would be an extension of the geological? Particularly in terms of the flow of stone?

AG: It is a way of accessing and understanding change, the broader meaning of change in a place, especially when you're confronted with a nostalgic desire to arrest change such as there is in the Cumbrian landscape. You realise the landscape is like it is because it has been changed, is being changed, will be changed. The introduction of contemporary art is an anathema to a lot of people in Cumbria. What I'm trying to do is also part of that change as cultural process.

TF: In both the **Sheepfolds Project**, and the **Refuges d'Art** project, there are layers – the cultural landscape, the agricultural, and also the geological. Certainly those two large projects provide a way for you to overlap geological and agricultural frames, but I think this is evident in earlier works such as **Rock Fold**, a commission you completed in 1993 in Dumfriesshire.

Rock Fold. Barfil, Dumfriesshire. 1993

AG: In all the landscapes that I work with, what I am really trying to understand is not just the materials that I can find – the isolated rock, the leaves – but also to see those materials as a way of understanding the rhythms of a landscape, and what flows through it. Gauging these movements in a landscape is critical to understanding it. Take that material that is considered the most stable, the measure of stability; stone. Granite, for instance, is considered more 'permanent' than most other stones. It doesn't have the softness of sandstone, but is itself a product of such profound change. It came from the ground as liquid, it is an igneous rock, formed by fire.

TF: What about those works where you take a boulder and enclose it in a building or structure? You talked about displacing large boulders as part of the **Drove Stones**. You also did it for the two sheepfolds at Mountjoy Farm and for **Garden of Stone** in New York. Doesn't enclosing such stones in this way contradict a sense of movement? How does enclosing a stone, or indeed a tree, sit with that notion of fluidity through the landscape?

AG: The stones for Garden of Stone at the Museum of Jewish Heritage in New York, had actually already been moved and placed to the sides of fields. So it was again very much in the spirit of agriculture and of

Garden of Stone
Museum of Jewish Heritage
New York
2003

the movement of them both geologically and agriculturally. The ones in Casterton were somewhat different. They would have been too large to be moved by the farmer, so had been left. The challenge for me has been to make my art deeper and more incisive. So the idea of taking a stone and putting it into a house or fold, as we did for Drove Stones, led to the far more interesting idea of taking the house to the stone, finding the stones in the place where they had come to rest. I didn't move or work the stone, other than change the context in which I found it; strangely, by enclosing it within a house.

TF: You are referring to **Stone House**?

AG: Yes. By encountering a boulder enclosed in a house, I would hope that you are made more aware of the journey it has made. I have used the term 'house' for previous work, and in ephemeral works. In Japan there was a large boulder that I made a stick/branch dome for. The branches don't touch the rock so it was very much like making a house for the stone. I did that as a way of understanding the relationship of the stone to the place in which it settled. These stones have made their surroundings their home. In Japan, my expectations were somewhat inverted, as typically between wood and stone, stone is taken to be the stronger partner.

There the mountains are so steep, so fragile, that the trees actually hold the mountains together. They are protecting the mountain. I love that inversion of what would be the normal idea of the relationship between the two. The glacial boulder that I found in Massachusetts was half buried, and I had it uncovered.

TF: Did you have it excavated?

AG: I found it in the woods. I guess it links to Rock Fold, which I made here in Dumfriesshire where, inside the fold, I removed the soil to reveal the bedrock.

TF: There is a process of revelation in both those works?

AG: Yes. It's a way of removing a layer, and revealing something that is there, but which to a large extent is hidden, or not understood, or acknowledged.

TF: **Rock Fold** is an interesting work. In Dumfriesshire, there is a thin skin that exists between the geological and the agricultural. There are visible outcrops of exposed bedrock everywhere. The layer of soil suddenly seems quite diaphanous, like a veil.

Opposite left:
Stone House. Asiho, Japan
7 November 1990

Opposite right:
In Asiho, Goldsworthy enclosed two boulders within wood domes. With the first of those, made on 6 November, Goldsworthy climbed in between the boulder and wood, recording the experience in a sequence of photographs.

Right:
Excavating the bedrock for Rock Fold.
Barfil, Dumfriesshire. 1993

AG: The notion of revealing and seeing what's there is very important to everything I do, from the ephemeral to the permanent. For instance, with the Chalk Stones commission. Sometimes what lies only a few inches or a foot or two below the surface is such a shock once it is revealed. In the case of chalk, it doesn't feel like it belongs there. When I placed large white boulders across the Sussex Downs, they looked so alien and yet right below the surface there is chalk. With the boulder in Massachusetts, the shock is that whilst it looks so much part of its place, it actually arrived there from elsewhere. So we excavated it to reveal its entirety. Just digging it out was quite a surprise. We then built a house for it. You don't know there's a stone in the house until you enter. It turns the stone into something else. With the Drove Stones, there is that sense of looking into the fold and half expecting to see a sheep sheltering inside bolt out. It is that expectation of movement…

TF: …a sense of energy, of nervousness.

Boulder 1. Chalk Stones. Sussex Downs. Installed 2002. Re-photographed 2006.

AG: On entering the house you see the stone, but I hope for one moment that you see it as something alive. It could feel extremely threatening because you can't walk around it. The stone forces you to press yourself between its surface and the wall of the house. The house is very dark; when you first go in you can't see your feet and there may be an animal in there. There are bears, snakes, raccoons, skunks, all manner of animals in the USA, which add to this sense of tension, and a feeling that something in that house is alive.

TF: The house becomes a mechanism for intensifying or amplifying the boulder. It is the viewer, the person who experiences, that is displaced.

AG: The whole perception of the rock changes because of the container, which is built around it. I think the series of recent 'houses' that I've been building have, in this respect, been far more successful than the sheepfolds because they are complete enclosures. When I made the dome to enclose the boulder in Japan, I found that crawling between the layers of skin of stone and skin of wood was a very interesting experience. The space around the stone becomes charged because it's contained. The Refuges in Digne, and the recent 'houses' even more so.

Left: excavating the boulder for Stone House. Massachusetts. 2005
Right: Stone House. Massachusetts. 2005

TF: With both **Rock Fold** and **Stone House**, you draw excavation into your process. However, it is not a process you use often. Obviously, excavation has archaeological references, and in Britain, there is an interface between the archaeological and the agricultural.

AG: I think I use excavation far more than you think. What is a black hole but excavation? Stone River at Stanford, for instance, is built into the ground. With those works, I excavate first. You feel as though you have revealed or exposed the space, and found something very archaeological. It does bring to the sculpture a powerful sense of 'was it something they dug out, was it always here or was it put there?' I love that. Putting things down into the ground so you would have to descend into it to see the sculpture: I see that having more mileage in my work in the future.

Stone River. Stanford University, California. 2001

TF: How interesting; I think it's a common perception of your work that it rests on the surface, and doesn't intervene or 'cut' into the land in the manner of some of the large interventions made by artists such as Michael Heizer, which have cut into the land, into the side of canyons. However, the notion of surface and space has always been there throughout your work hasn't it – with the hole, and then the hole/domes of the later 1980s?

AG: I've always been interested in penetrating the surface appearance of things, and the works do not just sit on the surface – they are rooted to the place they are made and grow out of those spaces. I resist the notion that my sculptures rest on the surface; I would like to think they connect, either visually or physically. However, I would probably draw the line about cutting into a valley or bedrock. I'm not ruling it out but it's something I feel reluctant to do. I will dig into the ground to reveal the bedrock, as I did with Rock Fold, and have always liked the idea of quarrying stone for a sculpture. So that is a moment where I would cut into it. I made a proposal for a large clay work for a stone quarry in Sydney where I was going to carve enclosures that would take clay works in the quarry bed. It was a brick pit so clay came out of it, that was its purpose – both stone and clay. So, in the context of the quarry, I'd be very happy to carve into the bedrock, but I would not cut into some interesting rock formation.

TF: I think the quarry is an interesting context for you, and where you have worked for a long time. In the same sense that you have referred to the farm as a human interface with the land, the quarry is a similar interface – with the geological if you like. Quarries are how we industrially 'farm' stone. And you have drawn parallels between the diaspora of people and a diaspora of stone across oceans as ballast to different countries. Do you think of the quarry as a socialised interface with the geological?

AG: Obviously a quarry relies heavily on the geology for the stone. It requires an understanding of the geology, the different qualities of stone that come out of it. There is a scale of quarrying, when surface coal is mined, where the place is just scraped away. I differentiate between those places, where a mountain has been levelled, and where there is a hole in a mountain that is a quarry. Sometimes these holes are huge, and are very powerful places. They also develop rich habitats once the quarrying has ended. I've worked in several places that have become protected, natural environments, because the quarry created a habitat that attracted a particular animal, and so made it richer than it was before.

TF: Robert Smithson reacted to what he saw as a picturesque response to extinct or former quarries; those that become overgrown and viewed as ruins in the landscape. You have particular views about the future of farming and the future of the British landscape as a farmed landscape. How do you feel about quarrying?

AG: There is nothing romantic about a working quarry – at all. They are brutal places to work in. After the work is finished, the dereliction and the growing over of the quarry are quite extraordinary. Now whether you romanticise that or not is neither here nor there, it's a fact. The quarry becomes a place that people look at as being beautiful in a way they didn't when it was working. However, the bigger challenge, if you like, is the dichotomy between people wanting stone for building purposes but not wanting the scar of the quarry in the landscape. I think this is a really important point in the way people relate to the landscape. The taking of material from a place can make it more interesting and richer. I would strongly resist the tendency that whenever there is excavation, there is a budget to reinstate, to cover up the quarry afterwards. There is a slate quarry at Ballachulish, which used to produce slate for Scotland. They spent a lot of money turning it into a park. I think the raw, overgrown quarry is a far more interesting place, and speaks more of the relationship between people and the land. Then there are quarries that people don't even see as being quarries – little cuts and holes. Near to my house, just a couple of hundred yards away in the field behind me, is a little bite out of the landscape, which probably produced stone for my house. To most people it looks like a natural outcrop, but it is in fact an excavated area of stone. The relationship between buildings and their origin is a very important one to me. Likewise, when I use wood in an installation such as I'm going to do at Yorkshire Sculpture Park or in Madrid later in 2007, people will see a massive amount of wood being used. However, for Yorkshire Sculpture Park, as with an exhibition I did at Albion Gallery in London in 2005, the wood comes from coppiced sources – where the taking of wood keeps the wood alive. It is part of ancient woodland that needs to be cut.

TF: The wood for the domed spaces, such as you installed at Albion, and will install at YSP, is from historic woodland?

AG: A woodland in Kent. Now, in Madrid I will be bringing an even greater amount of material into the Palacio di Cristal. People will go in and be shocked, and I'm sure there'll be a huge reaction to my using so much wood. The material is already cut down, lying in piles in woods near to Madrid, and comes from planted Scotch pine. It is on its way to the mills to be made into chipboard, which will in turn be used in the city. I'm going to take it, borrow it.

TF: You're extracting it out of a cycle.

AG: Yes it is part of a cycle, but what is interesting for me is when you present a material in its raw state, at its source, there is a shock and a sense of discomfort that people feel. If I were to bring the equivalent in chipboard and pile it up like minimalist sculptures about the space, there would be no shock. I try to confront that by going directly to the land: I use the stone there. I haven't ordered it through a stone yard. At best, my clay is dug from the ground, as it has been at Yorkshire Sculpture Park.

TF: The material is not mediated by a process or a system?

AG: Like meat and all the other things that we take for food, once it's been removed from its source and packaged it's somehow no longer...

TF: ... it's decontextualised?

AG: It has no longer come from the land; this is a very dangerous situation to be in. It makes people feel as if nature is somewhere else. What you use in the city is nature too, and I hope that when I make work in a building I succeed in making that association. When I cover one of the galleries at YSP with clay from the landscape, that is saying 'this building is earth'. The domes on the floor are saying, 'this floor is stone'. And the wood enclosure is saying, 'this building is wood'.

TF: That does draw us back to the series of 'houses' you mentioned, one of which, **Stone House**, we have discussed already. Could you also describe the work you made in California?

AG: After making Stone House, I went to Napa, in California, where I was asked to do a commission. There were a lot of oak trees, and one in particular had fallen down. It was next to a creek. It was collapsed on the ground, mostly intact, though there were bits broken off. This tree was so interesting, with lots of wonderful curvy branches. I stared

Constructing Falling Tree. Napa, California. 2005

and stared at the tree, wondering what I could do with it, and whether I could use the branches to make a woven stack ball or a column. I went through all these ideas, but the intention, as I've said previously, is to try and go underneath the surface, to push a little further, to use something of the place. And the place is not just the wood, it's the space. The idea came to me of building a house for the fallen tree.

TF: This strikes me as being about enclosure. Perhaps with **Stone House**, but I think much more consciously with **Falling Tree**, you were wanting to cradle the tree, which in effect is what the house does.

AG: For me, it feels as if the tree is falling through the house. We dug into the steep embankment upon which the tree had fallen to create space for the house to be built. It has a feeling of having been excavated, as if you are looking at a root or something that has always been there. It feels as though it's flowing or passing through. Although it is made permanent, and is rested in the house, the tree has a sense of falling, of being suspended. It has brought it back to that state and is about that act of collapse.

TF: Yes, there is something quite filmic about **Falling Tree**, a sense of the house structure merely freezing a frame. Compared with **Stone House**, **Falling Tree** has a much wider entrance, and as you view it from the road, it appears almost like a film still.

AG: It's like looking into a window of some kind. I purposely made a wide entranced front for it because I knew that, from a distance, you'd have that dark space with a tree floating in it. That only really works if you can see it from a distance, unlike Stone House, which is about proximity, being close up.

TF: Yes, they offer very different experiences. The boulder has a kind of brooding presence. **Stone House** has a feel of something welling up. With **Falling Tree**, the feeling is slightly different.

AG: They're both apertures into movement, glacial or decay. They're both about moving. To put a boulder or a fallen tree into a container somehow talks more about that movement than without it.

TF: In a sense you isolate it.

AG: It is that; but also 'how did it get here?', 'Why is it here?' Then you start thinking – because obviously the stone must have been put in afterwards – the entrance is too small for it to fit through.

TF: Defamiliarising is an interesting aspect of your work – with the chalk boulders and the glacial boulders. The sheepfold and then the 'house' have also become mechanisms to defamiliarise things.

AG: I do live in a house, and dealing with the house as a place, being indoors, is very important. I want an art that actually looks at all aspects of my life if possible. Stone House is interesting because the house lives with the stone rather than the people. The work is quite threatening and turns on its head what a house is for. Nonetheless, my houses examine our relationship to houses and shelters, where and how we seek shelter.

Constructing Falling Tree. Napa, California. 2005

TF: So you built **Falling Tree**, with a substantial oak that throws its limbs out into the built wall. This coincided with proposals you were developing for a permanent, site-specific work for Yorkshire Sculpture Park. You were invited to begin thinking about that process in 2004, and very quickly at YSP you were drawn to the partly derelict ha-ha, which goes around and through the Bretton Estate. Perhaps you can talk about how **Hanging Trees**, the commission that you finished in 2006 at YSP, came about.

AG: Well, in the spirit of the Sheepfolds Project, the Storm King Wall and the Wall that went for a walk, the idea of finding something that is in the landscape, perhaps hidden or derelict, that makes a connection to what was there before, is always of interest to me. YSP does have a ha-ha, which is actually at the perimeter of the formal grounds of Bretton Hall. So in effect the ha-ha is the interface between the grounds of the house and the surrounding agricultural landscape.

TF: Can you just clarify what a ha-ha is?

AG: A ha-ha is a wall within a ditch which prevents animals and sheep from coming into the garden. At the same time, it is not visible from the garden, so it feels as if the garden just flows into the wider landscape.

Section of derelict ha-ha at YSP. Potential site shot taken by Goldsworthy in 2005.

TF: To preserve the view from the house?

AG: In this instance, Bretton Hall. To me the ha-ha is part of what
has always felt like a very one-sided view of the landscape, an
uninterrupted idealistic view to be seen from the main house. The
landscape is designed and laid out for this one perspective, the
landowner's perspective. A little before YSP, I was asked to come
up with a proposal for Houghton in Norfolk where the ha-ha is
also employed. I discovered that Robert Walpole oversaw a lot of the
landscaping there and in the process removed an entire village and
levelled hills because they interrupted his view. There is a hugely
arrogant attitude attendant to this, wanting the place to appear perfect
from that perspective. To some extent this brings with it contemporary
attitudes towards the landscape. We are in a situation where people
often see the landscape as some pictorial backdrop to weekends spent
in the countryside. This is also a one-sided view. But of course there
are two sides – it's like stroking fur, there's a rough side and a smooth
side, along the grain and across the grain. Well I like the view from
across the grain, the rough side of it. I identify with the farmer in the
field, not the landowner in the house. There is also the view of up
close, in your hands, the grittiness of it, the earthiness of it. My initial

Aerial view of the Bretton Estate, showing Bretton Hall

ideas were to build something in the ha-ha at the same time as rebuild parts where it's derelict. This would integrate something that had to be seen from the other side; you would have to go over to the other side to look back and see these works.

TF: Yorkshire Sculpture Park incorporates within its grounds Bretton Hall and surrounding farmland, presenting you with a very interesting context. YSP has tenant farmers, which I think creates a dynamic that many other outdoor sculpture contexts lack. So often the farmer 'hosts' your work, if you like. At YSP, that relationship becomes complex. YSP has also given you, from one perspective, the first opportunity to work with what is really a piece of historic landscape, into which can be read layers of attitudes towards landscape. Are you aware that this is something you are getting to? Does it feel quite good or overdue to be dealing with this sort of landscape?

AG: It is good to be able to work with it, but I am seeing it from a contemporary perspective. It has all the ingredients that make, for me, the British landscape – all the reasons why Britain is the place in which my art grew. The equivalent context in the USA would be Storm King, privately owned, but publicly open as a sculpture park. It owns its own grounds, is very defined, and is very protected from its surroundings. The talk is always of preserving and protecting this place. YSP is very different; it was set up by Peter Murray when he was teaching at Bretton Hall during its time as an educational institution. He started putting sculpture in the grounds, and now the Sculpture Park is a large institution. Nonetheless, it has always had to coexist alongside other 'owners' – with the local Council, Leeds University, farmers. On Oxley Bank, where I built Hanging Trees, that particular part of the ha-ha is maintained by YSP. Directly on the other side is the farmer's land. There are all these wonderful tensions and difficulties of having to work in a social landscape, which are absent in a place like Storm King. Although it may make for an easier administrative ride for the sculpture there, I do love to rise to the challenge of all the resistances of a place like YSP. There is a feeling of real resistance of how to integrate the work into this space. Here in Britain we have always seemed to coexist with another institution or another landowner, and I think that social, human dimension to the landscape is far more part of the way artists like myself deal with the landscape. You cannot deal with the land without dealing with people.

TF: The **Sheepfolds Project** exemplified that of course: the fact that a landowner could put one of your sheepfolds into hiatus for three years. Perhaps that type of project couldn't have occurred in the States. Now in France it is occurring again with the **Refuges d'Art** project. The landscape, the elements with which you're working, means that you have different kinds of stakeholders working on the project, and that is, in part, what gives it extraordinary depth.

AG: Such spaces in the USA become state parks or national parks, which you drive to, whereupon you get out and walk in a protected environment. Whereas in Britain, the public rights of way lead you everywhere; people can have access to most places in some way. There are very few fields and hills that you cannot walk on, so even the landowners have to deal with the presence of people; they would prefer not to, but nonetheless people have a right to be there.

TF: At YSP you began to develop ideas, and you discovered that large parts of the ha-ha around Bretton Hall were underground, under earth, and what was visible above ground was probably four feet high? You dug down a bit and found that it went down to five and six feet at certain points. So the ha-ha itself is in part buried, partially in and out of view. You started thinking initially that you would make works in the ha-ha that were upright in the wall structure itself, didn't you?

AG: I have been visiting Yorkshire Sculpture Park for several years and I had begun to think of making some permanent and some ephemeral works embedded in the ha-ha. It would almost be like a gallery of works, sketches in the wall, and there were an awful lot of ideas I had been carrying around for a while. Certainly Napa was instrumental in opening up possibilities for Yorkshire Sculpture Park, as well as a group of ephemeral works I started making at the time that looked at the idea of enclosures and holes in the ground, or things that were embedded in the land. In particular I started working on a series of walls that I called the Burn Dam series.

TF: This was at Townhead Burn, near to your house?

AG: Yes, I dammed the stream with a wall and incorporated into the wall a wooden element comprised of dead elm branches. The series included six dams, all built successively downstream and eventually broken by flooding, by the rise in water.

TF: You would build them across the burn when the water was low. Then as the water rose, they began to dam up the stream. And they were frontally composed – to be seen from one perspective. The first of those incorporated a joined elm line, and then the next, which moved downstream, incorporated a woven ball. You are suggesting that they were primers for those first ideas for the ha-ha?

Windfallen dead Elm branch
sawn in two
worked into a wall
leaving a gap
through which the burn flowed
Townhead Burn, Dumfriesshire
7 January 2006

AG: The first two were before Yorkshire. But I was presented at Yorkshire with a very similar perspective – a raw, frontal view behind which is earth, and at Townhead Burn, water. I recall the water, the sense of it building up, the pressure building up behind. It was a fabulous kind of energy to have behind a wall – the feeling that the water might burst through. So, yes, these were current in my head.

TF: The commission that you went on to complete at YSP is horizontal and built into the ground. You made three large chambers within the run of the ha-ha, not the ha-ha that you were first exploring which was quite close to Bretton Hall, but further away, up on Oxley Bank. Your initial proposals had been frontal. You were thinking of building something into the wall, which would be experienced face-on. Was it the piece at Napa, **Falling Tree**, that made you move from the upright to the horizontal, to the big troughs in the ground?

AG: I'm not sure where the idea first came from, but I do remember a point where I made the work at Napa. I also had a show at Galerie Lelong in Paris, and I was making work at Townhead Burn: in the pile of stones at the side of the burn I built chambers or openings, into which I put first a branch, then a ball of branches, and then a branch line. Funnily enough, pivotal to all that was a commission at Cap d'Antibes years ago, which never came to fruition. I remember that there was a well at the property and a hole into the ground where you looked down. Wells are fascinating things, frightening and unnerving. You don't know how deep they are, and there's always a sense of falling when I look into them. At some point that all came together in Falling Tree, and the thought that if I placed a tree in a well that the outstretched limbs would echo your own sensation of possibly falling into that space. The prone tree, floating, moving…

TF: There's something quite terrifying about a prone tree.

AG: There is, held there in a state of suspension. As with Napa, the sense of opening a space and finding the body of a tree there, of revealing something. That, for me, was a far stronger sculptural

Elm branches
Townhead Burn, Dumfriesshire
15-16 January 2006

expression of these ideas than sticking something into the wall, as though it was some sort of picture. And everything fell into place.

TF: So you found collapsed parts of the ha-ha?

AG: Yes, on Oxley Bank. Unusually for a ha-ha it is a two-sided wall. This differentiates it from the stretch that surrounds Bretton Hall. The ha-ha at Oxley Bank is a concealed wall because a ditch had been dug along the brow of the hill. They didn't want to have a wall visible on the hill from the main house, so they dug the long ditch in which the ha-ha sits. A huge amount of work would have been required to build the wall in the middle of the ditch so that it couldn't be seen. It is freestanding, and this means that I had two sides of the wall to work with, that I could open up enclosures within derelict areas. I chose three derelict sections, we dug into the ground, and these fairly large rectangles with trees suspended in them are now made. It also means that part of the work is on the farmer's side, part is on YSP's side.

TF: **Hanging Trees** very literally gives a view into the landscape, rather than revealing the landscape as a kind of text.

AG: Also the ha-ha is another example of the tension between wood and stone, especially in the form of the wall. The wood is pressing, attacking and gnawing at the stone, you can see it is derelict because roots have pushed it apart. There is tremendous tension on the line of the wall, and I think by incorporating the tree it's another part of that tension that is inevitable on boundaries and borders, be they geological, between the sea and coast, or the river and riverbank. It focuses on that wonderful transition – no, not a transition – a flashpoint of friction between two elements.

TF: Those trenches are ten feet deep. The structures are embedded in the land so that each enclosure is subterranean. From the point of view of the visitor, as you walk up to the structures you don't actually see what is in there until you're almost on top looking down into them. For me, walking up to Oxley Bank, on the approach to **Hanging Trees**, there is a resonance with Gustave Courbet's painting **Burial at Ornans** Perhaps it is the high horizon line in that painting, and the open hole in the ground into which you can't see. Courbet's landscape is tiered – it is very compressed. The open grave is at the feet of the individuals, but it is they who seem buried. In what way do you feel that those enclosures have that aspect – of a sarcophagus perhaps?

AG: They are both; they are resting places for the trees. You wonder whether the tree is growing out of the enclosure or whether it is a place for it to decay. I think ultimately for me, it is both. Those two things are intertwined: the openings show growth, the tree is growing inside the ground, and there's the pressure and energy of growth. In Townhead Burn, I work with elm trees that have died because of Dutch elm disease. It is a small stretch of woodland around a very small stream which is littered with decaying and fallen trees. And it has that sense of layering you speak of in relation to Burial at Ornans, starting with the treetops and then the collapsing down of those trees – there is a compression as these things fall into the river. There is a huge sense of death and decay in the Burn. It's a very grim place in some ways, and yet the death of all these trees has such a lively impact on the materials I can work with, and the stream itself. There are dams and small waterfalls all along the stream, and they are rich and wet, where branches and bits of bark clog up and intertwine. The burn is very much alive because of the death of the trees. If I work there another twenty or thirty years will there be any more elm trees left? Eventually they will have all fallen and rotted away, and the stream will revert to this quiet piece of water. Actually the death and disease that has occurred there has made it a traumatically interesting place to work. That's how I want to see the landscape; I don't want to see it as this calm, pastoral, beautiful thing. I want to see it for what it really is. It's a very challenging place to be. When I went through a couple of months of very difficult personal time, I worked in Townhead Burn every day. When that time reached a certain conclusion there was a flood. I went back to the Burn and all the places I'd worked had been scoured away, so it started again. The whole cycle of my work started again, it was a shock to see those constants suddenly ripped away.

ANDY GOLDSWORTHY
AT YORKSHIRE SCULPTURE PARK:
A VISUAL RECORD OF THE
EXHIBITION AND ITS MAKING

UNDERGROUND GALLERY
NEW WORK

Stacked Oak
Branches left over from trees
That were being felled locally
Collected during the installation
Supplied by Job Earnshaw and Bros Ltd
2007

self-supporting structure

Stone Room
Yorkshire sandstone
Quarried by Johnson's Wellfield, Huddersfield
Dry stone construction
Carved holes
2007

11 domes
55 tons of Yorkshire sandstone

Clay Room
Clay dug from the grounds of Yorkshire Sculpture Park
Dried, sieved, mixed with human hair
Reconstituted and applied to the gallery walls
Many participants
2007

20 tons of clay
300 litres of human hair
180 m^2 surface area
over 60 volunteers

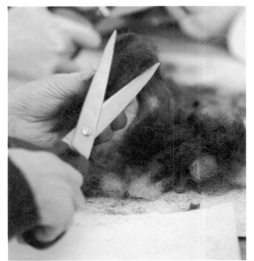

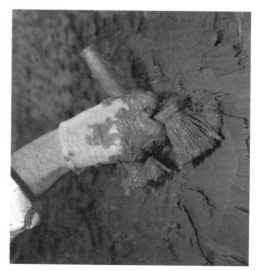

Wood Room
Coppiced Sweet Chestnut
Cropped from woodland in Kent
A process by which limbs are cut, and then regrow
2007

760 logs
self-supporting structure

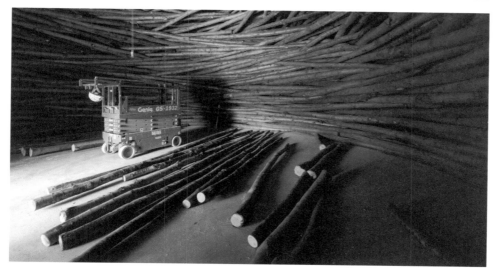

Leaf Stalk Room
Horse Chestnut leaf stalks
Collected from trees in and around Yorkshire Sculpture Park
Held together with Blackthorns
2007

10,500 leaf stalks

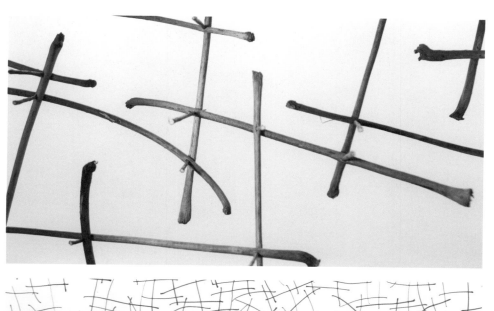

123

Striding Arches
self-supporting
Locharbriggs red sandstone
Quarried by Marshalls, Dumfries
En route to Cairnhead Forest, Dumfriesshire
2006-2008

LONGSIDE GALLERY:
SHEEP PAINTINGS
MUD BALL
COW DUNG ON GLASS

Sheep paintings
Yorkshire Sculpture Park
2006

Mud trailed into the YSP Centre and Longside Gallery
swept up and made into a ball
beginning 1 March 2007
to be continued for the duration of the exhibition
2007-8

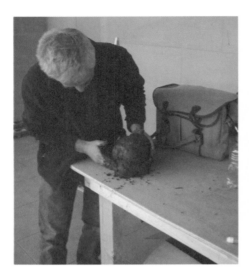

Cow dung on glass
2007

Dung collected from the dairy cattle
of YSP tenant farmer Philip Platts

137

NEW WORK IN THE LANDSCAPE

Hanging Trees
Upper sections of oaks
Being felled locally
Supplied by Job Earnshaw
Oxley Bank
Yorkshire Sculpture Park
2006

Outclosure
Round Wood
Yorkshire sandstone
Quarried by Johnson's Wellfield, Huddersfield
Sited with permission of Job Earnshaw and Bros Ltd
Yorkshire Sculpture Park
2007

Shadow Stone Fold
Yorkshire sandstone
Quarried by Johnson's Wellfield, Huddersfield
Built on site of old fold
Yorkshire Sculpture Park
2007

GLOSSARY

STORM KING

Established in 1960, Storm King Art Center is in Mountainville, New York State. Five hundred acres of landscaped lawns, fields and woodlands provide the site for postwar sculptures by internationally renowned artists. Much of the open area at Storm King was farmed for more than two hundred years, until the first half of the twentieth century when agriculture in the Hudson Valley became harder to sustain.

GRIZEDALE

The Grizedale sculpture trail in the Lake District National Park was set up in 1977. In its early years, Grizedale focused on environmental and land art, with artists making work within the forest. In recent times its focus has shifted to artists' residencies and wider engagement with issues concerning the relationship between the rural and urban dichotomy in Cumbria.

DAVID NASH'S CAE'N-Y-COED

Four acres of woodland in the Vale of Ffestiniog which David Nash inherited from his father. The first living artwork Nash made there in 1977 was Ash Dome, a circle of ash saplings which he has tended ever since, using traditional hedging methods, pruning and training, to form a five metre high domed space.

KENTUCK KNOB

Kentuck Knob in western Pennsylvania was designed by Frank Lloyd Wright in the last decade of his career for the Hagen family, and completed in 1956. In 1986 it was sold to Lord Peter Palumbo who opened the house and grounds to the public in 1996. It features a sculpture meadow.

ILE DE VASSIVIÈRE

A seventy five hectare island on a vast man-made lake in the Limoges region of France. Located on the island is the International Centre of Art and the Landscape, designed by Aldo Rossi. The island is used for the siting of outdoor sculpture and site-specific commissions.

RÉSERVE GÉOLOGIQUE DE HAUTE-PROVENCE, FRANCE

The Réserve Géologique is regarded as Europe's biggest geological open-air museum, with its base in Digne-Les-Bains. Created in 1984, its total protection area now incorporates 200,000 hectares of the southern Alps, 55 communities, and at least 18 geological sites of the carboniferous period that date to approximately 300 million years ago. Since 1995, the Réserve, together with Musée Gassendi, has commissioned contemporary artists to undertake projects within its territories, which have resulted in both permanent and temporary works.

ANDY GOLDSWORTHY

Born in Cheshire in 1956, Andy Goldsworthy is known internationally for his
outdoor ephemeral sculptures and permanent installations. Goldsworthy's
experience of 'materials in place' has evolved over thirty years. With his ephemeral
practice, he uses whatever natural materials and weather conditions are to be
encountered at the place of making, and makes short-lived, often formal works of
tension and intensity. As a counterpoint, Goldsworthy's permanent commissions
engage predominantly with the layered and encultured history of land use,
frequently through agricultural and geological frames of reference, such as farming
and quarrying. Sheepfolds Project (1996-2007, Cumbria) and Refuges d'Art (1999
onwards, Réserve Géologique de Haute-Provence, France) are his most sustained
and multi-layered explorations of those concerns.

Goldsworthy has also undertaken large-scale ephemeral projects in urban contexts,
such as Snowballs in Summer (London, 2000), as well as gallery-based installations
such as White Walls (New York, 2007). Recent and current projects include: Roof
(2004-5), National Gallery of Art, Washington DC; Drawn Stone (2005) De Young,
Museum, San Francisco; Striding Arches (2004-), Cairnhead, Dumfriesshire; Hanging
Trees (2006), Yorkshire Sculpture Park.

Goldsworthy studied at Bradford College of Art (1974-1975) and Preston Polytechnic
(Lancaster Annex) (1975-1978). He has lived and worked in Dumfriesshire for over
twenty years.

TINA FISKE

Dr Tina Fiske is an art historian, and teaches at the History of Art Department,
University of Glasgow. She is also co-Director of Bracker Fiske contemporary art
consultancy. Tina has recently overseen the completion of the Andy Goldsworthy
Digital Catalogue Volume 1: 1976-1986, which documents the first ten years of
Goldsworthy's ephemeral work: www.cc.gla.ac.uk/goldsworthy. She is also
currently compiling a catalogue of Goldsworthy's permanent works and
commissions for a forthcoming publication for the National Gallery of Art,
Washington DC (2008).

SELECTED PUBLICATONS

Dates given are for the first edition, unless stated otherwise.

Enclosure (2007), London: Thames and Hudson; New York: Abrams; Frankfurt-am-Main: Zweitausendeins (with James Putnam)

Passage (2004), London: Thames and Hudson; New York: Abrams; Arcueil: Anthese; Warnsveld: Terra (texts by Simon Schama, Richard Dorment, Anne L Strauss, Susan L Talbot, Chris Gilbert, Dede Young and Stephanie Hanor et al.)

Refuges d'Art (2002), France: Editions Artha (with text by Nadine Gomez and Irene Magnaudex)

Mid-Summer Snowballs (2001), London: Thames and Hudson; New York: Abrams; Frankfurt-am-Main: Zweitausendeins (with Judith Collins)

Time (2000), London: Thames and Hudson; New York: Abrams; Frankfurt-am-Main: Zweitausendeins; Arcueil: Anthese; Warnsveld: Terra (chronology by Terry Friedman)

Arch (1999), London: Thames and Hudson; New York: Abrams; Frankfurt-am-Main: Zweitausendeins; Arcueil: Anthese (with David Craig)

Wall (1998), London: Thames and Hudson; New York: Abrams; Frankfurt-am-Main: Zweitausendeins; Arcueil: Anthese (with Kenneth Baker and additional photography by Jerry Thompson)

Cairns (1997), France: Digne-Les-Bains

Wood (1996), London: Viking; New York: Abrams; Arcueil: Anthese; Warnsveld: Terra (with Terry Friedman)

Sheepfolds (1996), London: Michael Hue-Williams Fine Art Ltd (with Steve Chettle, Andrew Humphries and Paul Nesbitt)

Stone (1994), London: Viking; New York: Abrams; Arcueil: Anthese; Warnsveld: Terra

Two Autumns (1993), London and Japan: Togichi Prefectural Museum of Fine Arts and Setagaya Art Museum

Hand to Earth (1st ed. 1991, 2nd ed. 2004), (1st ed.) Leeds: Henry Moore Centre for the Study of Sculpture; (2nd ed.) London: Thames and Hudson; New York: Abrams (with Terry Friedman, Miranda Strickland-Constable, Andrew Causey, Paul Nesbitt, Hans Vogel, Sue Clifford and Angela King, Clive Adams et al.)

Touching North (1989), London and Edinburgh: Fabian Carlsson and Graeme Murray

Leaves (1989), London: Common Ground

Parkland (1st ed. 1987, 2nd ed. 2007), Wakefield: Yorkshire Sculpture Park

Rain sun snow hail mist calm: Photo works by Andy Goldsworthy (1985), Leeds and Sunderland: The Henry Moore Centre for the Study of Sculpture, Leeds City Art Gallery and Northern Centre for Contemporary Art, Sunderland

PHOTOGRAPHY CREDITS

Cover, pp2-4 + p12: **Jonty Wilde**

Interview illustrations:
Andy Goldsworthy, except pp24-25: John Goldsworthy, and pg 74: Jonty Wilde

All other images listed by page number and then numbered sequentially from top left, reading left to right.

p82: **Jonty Wilde**

p85: 1, 2 + 5: **Jonty Wilde**, 3 + 4: **Jacob Ehrenberg**

p86: 1, 2 + 4: **Jonty Wilde**, 3 + 5 **Jacob Ehrenberg**

p87: **Jacob Ehrenberg**

pp88-89: **Jonty Wilde**

p91: **Jonty Wilde**

p92: 1, 3, 4 + 5: **Jonty Wilde**, 2: **Jacob Ehrenberg**

p93: **Jonty Wilde**

p94: 1, 2, 3 + 4: **Jonty Wilde** 5: **Jacob Ehrenberg**

p95: 1: **Jacob Ehrenberg**, 2 + 3: **Jonty Wilde**

pp96-97: **Jonty Wilde**

p99: 1 + 4: **Alan Mackenzie**, 2 + 5: **Dick Ellis**, 3: **Helen Pheby**

p100: 1, 3 + 5: **Jonty Wilde**, 2 + 4: **Dick Ellis**

pp101-102: **Jonty Wilde**

p103: 1 + 2: **Jonty Wilde**, 3 + 4: **Dick Ellis**

p104: **Jonty Wilde**

p105:1, 3 + 5: **Jonty Wilde**, 2 + 4: **Dick Ellis**

p106: 1 + 3: **Jonty Wilde**, 2, 4 + 5: **Jacob Ehrenberg**

p107: **Jonty Wilde**

pp108-109: **Jonty Wilde**

pp111-113: **John Paul Bland**

p114: 1 + 4: **Jacob Ehrenberg**, 2+3: **Dick Ellis**

p115: 1 + 4: **Jonty Wilde**, 2: **Dick Ellis** 3: **Jacob Ehrenberg**

p116: 1 + 4: **Jonty Wilde**, 2, 3 + 5: **Dick Ellis**

p117: **Jonty Wilde**

pp118-119: **Jonty Wilde**

p121: 1 + 4: **Jonty Wilde**, 2: **Helen Pheby**, 3: **Jacob Ehrenberg**

p122: 1 + 2: **Jacob Ehrenberg**, 3: **Jonty Wilde**

pp123-128: **Jonty Wilde**

p129: **Andy Goldsworthy**

pp131-132: **Sarah Coulson**

p133: **Jonty Wilde**

p134: 1 + 2: **Jacob Ehrenberg**, 3: **Jonty Wilde**

p135: **Jonty Wilde**

p136: 1 + 2: **Jonty Wilde**, 3, 4 + 5: **Jacob Ehrenberg**

pp137-140: **Jonty Wilde**

pp142-145: **Alan Mackenzie**

pp146-149: **Jonty Wilde**

p150: 1 + 4: **Jacob Ehrenberg**, 2 + 3: **Jonty Wilde**

pp151-153: **Jonty Wilde**

p154: 1: **Andy Goldsworthy**, 2 + 3: **Jonty Wilde**

p155: **Jonty Wilde**

p156: 1, 2 + 3: **Jonty Wilde**, 4: **Jacob Ehrenberg**, 5: **Andy Goldsworthy**

p157: 1 + 2 : **Jonty Wilde**, 3 + 4: **Jacob Ehrenberg**

p158: **Jonty Wilde**

p159: **Alan Mackenzie**

ANDY GOLDSWORTHY WOULD LIKE TO THANK:

Peter Murray and Roger Evans.

Alan Mackenzie, Clare Lilley, Helen Pheby, Sarah Coulson, Jane Marshall,
Johanna McTiernan, Iain Stephenson, Jan Wells, Anna Bowman, Joff Whitten,
James Standaloft, Neil Lingwood, Ian Fallon, Sam Clayton, Mark Jacobs, Mark
Chesman, Claire Midwood, Ian Fisher, Anna Neville, Vic Darley, Anthony Shepherd,
Matt Bertola, Rob Grant, Shaun Pickard, Simon Skirrow, Dick Ellis, Heather Toulson,
Helen Toulson, Philippa Higgins, Janice Doherty, the volunteers who helped install
Clay Room, and all the staff at YSP.

Jacob Ehrenberg, Eric Sawden, Tina Fiske, Steve Allen, Gordon Wilton,
Bill Noble, Jason Wilton, Andy Mason, Mark Heathcote, Dave Griffiths,
Nigel Goody, John Billington, Simon Lumb, Alistair Lumb, Christopher Lumb.

Philip Platts, Graham Mallinson, Job Earnshaw & Sons, Sid and Chubb Weston,
Brian Buckley, D Gemmell and Sons.

Jan Hogarth, Brian Nish, George Rennie and Cairnhead Community Trust.
Charlie Meecham and Spectrum. Jonty Wilde. John Paul Bland. Tim Blake and Paul
Tame at John Jones. Ian Taylor and his students. Rose Cooper and her students.

Michael Hue-Williams, Cheryl Haines, Mary Sabbatino,
Jean Frémon, and Auguste Hoviele.

Published by Yorkshire Sculpture Park to coincide with the exhibition

ANDY GOLDSWORTHY
31 March 2007 – 6 January 2008
Underground, Longside, Bothy and Garden Galleries, and open air

Exhibition generously sponsored by Roger Evans
with support from the Henry Moore Foundation

ISBN   1 871480 60 4

Editing and image selection: Sarah Coulson, Tina Fiske and Andy Goldsworthy
Design and production: Sarah Coulson
Printed in the UK by Derek Hattersley & Son, Barnsley